DRAWN TO THE FLAME:
ASSESSMENT AND TREATMENT OF
JUVENILE FIRESETTING BEHAVIOR

Robert F. Stadolnik, EdD

FirePsych, Inc.
Norwood, Massachusetts

Professional Resource Press
Sarasota, Florida

Published by
Professional Resource Press
(An imprint of the Professional Resource Exchange, Inc.)
Post Office Box 15560
Sarasota, FL 34277-1560

Printed in the United States of America

The copy editor for this book was David Anson, the managing editor was Debbie Fink, and the production coordinator was Laurie Girsch.

Library of Congress Cataloging-in-Publication Data

Stadolnik, Robert F., date.
    Drawn to the flame : assessment and treatment of juvenile firesetting behavior / Robert F. Stadolnik.
        p. cm. -- (Practitioner's resource series)
    Includes bibliographical references.
    ISBN 1-56887-063-9 (alk. paper)
    1. Pyromania in children. 2. Fire behavior in children. 3. Arson. 4. Child psychotherapy. I. Title. II. Series.

RJ506.P95 S83 2000
618.92'85843--dc21

                                                00-040310

DEDICATION

In Memory of
Chief John J. Sheehy
1942-1996
Westwood Fire Department
Westwood, Massachusetts

A man whose leadership, dedication, and selfless
commitment to the protection of children and families
and the men who served with him was inspirational to so many of us.
With his great respect for fire's inherent danger and his
vigilant dedication to preparedness, protection, and
prevention, he saved lives.

SERIES PREFACE

As a publisher of books, audio- and videotapes, and continuing education programs, the Professional Resource Press and Professional Resource Exchange, Inc. strive to provide mental health professionals with highly applied resources that can be used to enhance clinical skills and expand practical knowledge.

All the titles in the Practitioner's Resource Series are designed to provide important new information on topics of vital concern to psychologists, clinical social workers, marriage and family therapists, psychiatrists, and other mental health professionals.

Although the focus and content of each book in this series will be quite different, there will be notable similarities:

1. Each title in the series will address a timely topic of critical clinical importance.
2. The target audience for each title will be practicing mental health professionals. Our authors were chosen for their ability to provide concrete "how-to-do-it" guidance to colleagues who are trying to increase their competence in dealing with complex clinical problems.
3. The information provided in these books will represent "state-of-the-art" information and techniques derived from both clinical experience and empirical research. Each of these guide books will include references and resources for those who wish to pursue more advanced study of the discussed topics.
4. The authors will provide numerous case studies, specific recommendations for practice, and the types of "nitty-gritty" details that clinicians need before they can incorporate new concepts and procedures into their practices.

We feel that one of the unique assets of the Professional Resource Press is that all of its editorial decisions are made by mental health professionals. The publisher, all editorial consultants, and all reviewers are practicing psychologists, marriage and family therapists, clinical social workers, and psychiatrists.

If there are other topics you would like to see addressed in this series, please let me know.

Lawrence G. Ritt, Publisher

ABSTRACT

Children and adolescents are responsible, either intentionally or accidentally, for an alarmingly high percentage of the tremendous fire problem that exists in the United States. Their firesetting behavior accounts for nearly half of all structure fires along with a major portion of the thousands of fire fatalities and severe burn injuries that occur each year. Despite the prevalence of this behavior, juvenile firesetting has received little attention in mental health literature and research. Many mental health professionals remain entrenched in, and limited by, long-held beliefs about firesetting behavior that are more mythologically than factually based.

Juvenile firesetting is an often complex and inherently dangerous behavior that involves a diverse population of children who display a heterogeneous set of emotional, behavioral, and environmental characteristics. Successful intervention with firesetting behavior requires the ability to coordinate a multidisciplinary array of services — including mental health treatment — that addresses the often unique and complicated needs of each child or adolescent.

This work comprehensively cites the relevant research and findings and provides the mental health practitioner with a description of the assessment domains, models, and tools that currently represent "best practice" standards in the field of juvenile firesetting behavior. In addition, it describes the importance of collaboration with fire service professionals and identifies numerous regional, state, and national resources for those interested in pursuing further study, training, and skill development.

TABLE OF CONTENTS

DRAWN TO THE FLAME:
ASSESSMENT AND TREATMENT OF JUVENILE FIRESETTING BEHAVIOR

INTRODUCTION

Fire is fascinating. It is physically both powerful and beautiful. Throughout history, man has learned to use and manipulate fire in an almost incomprehensible number of ways. Throughout the ages, man has used fire to conquer and defend, to build and destroy, and to celebrate and mourn. From the Middle Ages to the Industrial Revolution, and from the Cold War to the race to the moon, man's destiny has been largely determined by the ability to manipulate and control fire. Fire, it could be argued, is one of the most powerful and influential elements in the universe.

It is widely accepted in archeological circles that primitive man discovered fire approximately half a million years ago. This discovery, whether accidental or intentional, was the precise moment at which our existence and dominance as a species was assured. Man, comparably weak in relation to other animals, suddenly became capable of dominating every other species and his physical environment as well. Primitive man's ability to make and use fire set the human race apart from every other creature on God's good earth.

Today, fire remains a significant part of our everyday lives. It heats our homes, cooks our food, fuels our cars, powers our machinery, and detonates our weapons. It has a prominent place in our religious and secular customs. Despite the facts that we are impacted by fire every day and that our existence literally depends on it, we remain a culture that has yet to become truly comfortable with fire. Would it surprise

1

you to know that most adults are unable to answer the most basic of questions about fire? Could you define fire if asked? When you understand fire as the chemical chain reaction of combustion, involving the rapid oxidation of a fuel, you are able to appreciate and understand why it is inherently uncontrollable. Can you name the three elements of the "fire triangle" — those three elements (heat, fuel, air) necessary to initiate and sustain the chemical chain reaction of combustion (fire) and which provide the basic foundation for the study of fire suppression? How could something so important and constant in our lives be so distant from us that we don't even know what it is and what it needs to survive?

The truth is that our relationship with fire is not only distant but also quite distorted. A quick look at our media advertising reveals our tendency to "eroticize" this chemical chain reaction. Adjectives such as "hot," "smoldering," and "burning" are more commonly used to describe states of sexual excitement than states of combustion. Images of flame and smoke are seen more often in advertisements for perfumes and cars than in public messages on fire safety. We have fallen madly in love with fire and, in order to do so, we have distanced ourselves from the inherent danger it poses.

Television, movies, cartoons, and video games are full of examples of all types of explosions and incendiary events that never seem to do the kind of damage a real fire does. How often could Wiley Coyote, of *Roadrunner* fame, become vaporized by the accidental detonation of one of his creations from his favorite bomb-making company, the ACME Co.? A Saturday spent watching animated television exposes one to dozens of incendiary explosions that inflict damages that magically disappear for the next scene. Today's action movies consistently depict heroes and heroines escaping through fires and explosions that would produce enough heat to destroy human lung and skin tissue in a matter of seconds.

As a result of being bombarded with these unrealistic, sanitized images of fire and having few real opportunities to interact with fire in a responsible and purposeful way, we are fast becoming a species that is growing more distant from one of the very elements that has defined us throughout history.

Considering the sensationalized exposure to fire to which we have subjected our children via the media and the personal qualities ascribed to fire during the past generation, it is not surprising that juveniles, too, are fascinated and intrigued by fire and drawn to its properties. How many families have brought their children, especially sons, to visit the fire station to see the trucks and the firemen? How many birthday candles do our children blow out in the course of a lifetime? How many professional fireworks displays, campfires, or beach bonfires do we attend with our children? Yet many adults, professionals included, perceive a child's fascination with fire and interest in playing with fire as unusual, uncomfortable, or even deviant.

While in its simplest form this reaction might seem odd, it is easy to understand how this has come to pass. The fact of the matter is that since early man discovered fire nearly half a million years ago in the caves of modern day Asia, it has been used in ways that are irresponsible, destructive, and often intentionally harmful. Ever since prehistoric times, fire has been the only weapon of mass destruction that is easily available to every member of the species. And, with that availability, has come a host of problems.

While understandable given the greater cultural context, our reactions to a child's or an adolescent's attraction to, and irresponsible use of, fire creates several problems that have grown to significant levels during the past several decades. Within the mental health and social service disciplines, there exist numerous myths and misperceptions about juvenile firesetting behavior. The influence of these myths has often limited or prohibited the availability of intervention services to these juveniles and their families — services that could have a direct impact on risk for future firesetting behavior. Worse yet there exists, among lay persons and child and adolescent mental health professionals, a lack of awareness of the problem's existence. One factor that contributes to the pervasive lack of knowledge in the mental health field regarding juvenile firesetting behavior is the lack of an adequate body of written data on the topic (Fineman, 1995; Geller, 1992; Kolko, 1985). We simply do not know enough about this behavior because resources have not been devoted to study it in a systematic way.

Currently the study of firesetting behavior is severely limited by the following factors:

1. *Lack of an adequate body of research data.* The total number of pieces of credible research sources on juvenile firesetting behaviors is *less than 300*. This compares to the thousands of research studies on eating disorders, depression, anxiety disorders, and sexual abuse.

2. *Absence of a clear and widely accepted definition of firesetting.* At the heart of the matter is the fact that there is disagreement as to which parameters (the criteria which define) define a "firesetter." Is it the frequency of the behavior? Is it the severity of the resultant fire? Is it related to the child's or adolescent's

intent or motivation for the behavior? The studies that do exist are utilizing selection criteria that are vastly different from one another.

3. *Small and homogeneous study populations.* Many studies are limited to populations of 10 to 20 juveniles who are actually representative of subpopulations of juveniles who are involved in firesetting behavior. Very few studies have involved nonclinical populations of juveniles.

4. *Lack of an objective measure of the behavior.* The tools available to help a clinician determine the severity level of firesetting behavior are highly subjective and depend largely upon the experience, clinical interview skills, and fire knowledge level of the examiner.

5. *Limited access to the population.* It is widely accepted that only 20% to 25% of the total population of juveniles who have engaged in firesetting behavior is actually brought to the attention of fire service or mental health professionals.

What you are about to read in this book may surprise or even shock you. My experience has been that even those professionals who have worked with children and adolescents for long periods of time are often quite taken aback, or are intellectually skeptical, when they are presented with the statistical and clinical information on the extent of the firesetting problem we face in this country. This reaction is in many ways the result of the fact that most major training programs have not incorporated this information into their curriculum or their opportunities for practicum/internship experience.

The purpose of this book is to provide psychologists, mental health professionals, and social service professionals with an accurate and detailed picture of the fire problem that currently exists in our country and the extent to which children and adolescents are responsible. This book will also review and explain the history of the development of the prevailing juvenile firesetting mythology, which then will be contrasted with accurate incidence and prevalence data and current research-based diagnostic and demographic information.

The book will present an organized and detailed description of the domains that are typically included in the completion of a firesetting behavior assessment. I will discuss several examples of the assessment models, tools, and instruments most commonly used by professionals across the country. In addition, the book will outline a description of the practical use and application of various treatment strategies.

RESEARCH FACTS VERSUS
COMMON FICTION: UNDERSTANDING
THE JUVENILE FIRESETTING PROBLEM

When given the opportunity to work with children and adolescents engaged in firesetting behaviors, many mental health professionals commonly experience a sense of intellectual conflict and confusion. As they begin to gather clinical information, this new information collides with previously held, fundamental beliefs about the etiology, diagnostic characteristics, and negative treatment prognosis that the term "firesetting" creates. Eyes will roll, heads will shake solemnly, and shoulders will recoil as if to say "That's too bad" in an empathetic tone. Some will say with an air of confidence, "Oh, a pyro," referring to the diagnostic category of Pyromania found among the Impulse-Control Disorders of the *Diagnostic and Statistical Manual of Mental Disorders* (*DSM-IV*; American Psychiatric Association [APA], 1994). If there were ever a diagnostic term that is misused as a part of our everyday language, one could make a strong argument for "pyromania" as that diagnosis. Yet the overwhelming majority of professionals in the field of child and adolescent mental health have never been given the opportunity in their undergraduate, graduate, or internship/practicum experiences to study firesetting behavior in a meaningful way. It is difficult, if not impossible, to find a graduate training program that offers a course, or even a portion of a behavioral disorders course, that comprehensively addresses firesetting behavior. Most of the major behavioral disorder or child and adolescent psychology textbooks used in our strongest training programs include only secondary references to juvenile firesetting.

Where then have we gathered our base of information? Many of us may have had anecdotal case experiences in which firesetting was seen as a symptom of the "real problem" and was therefore relegated to secondary status in terms of direct treatment. Others hear of the clinical experiences of peers and supervisors who, depending on their personal and professional experiences, develop highly personalized conceptual interpretations of the behavior and, as a result, design treatment strategies that are more reflective of their body of experiences than the relevant body of literature.

Worse yet, as professionals we are not immune from the influence of the media, written and electronic, which tends to present *all* problematic behaviors, including firesetting, in as sensationalized a portrayal as possible. As a result of these factors and the lack of adequate and reliable data mentioned earlier, there has developed a rather extensive set of prevailing myths among professionals and lay people relative to firesetting behavior among juveniles. Tragically, it is these prevailing myths that often are the driving forces behind the assessment formulations and treatment decisions made for juveniles and families as the result of their involvement in a fire-related incident.

Several years ago I had the opportunity to assess an 11-year-old boy named Jeremy,* who had spent the previous year in residential treatment as a result of his having, according to a hospital admissions chart, "burned his house to the ground." This one notation was cited in almost every subsequent evaluation, progress note, summary report, and consultation note. What his treatment providers neglected to do, or more accurately were unable to do, was to skillfully interview him about the fire and his actions of that day. If they had, they would have discovered that on that Saturday afternoon Jeremy had been attempting to light a teddy bear on fire, inside a metal mixing bowl, under his bed because "my father wouldn't play with me." What he didn't realize was that the underside of his bed would ignite as a result of the heat generated by the teddy bear. He made several efforts to put the fire out with cups of water from the bathroom while yelling for his father's help. Unfortunately, Jeremy's intoxicated father had passed out on the couch downstairs and awoke only in time to get himself out of the house safely. An anxious child by nature, Jeremy was so distraught during the aftermath of the fire that he presented as quite "out of control" and "disorganized" according to hospital records. Who wouldn't be? Jeremy was admitted that afternoon and spent the next 2 months in the hospital before being placed in a long-term residential program. No one ever asked him about the fire and his fire behaviors were never a specific focus of treatment. Unfortunately, situations like this, where the size of the fire is used to determine motivation, are far too commonplace and result in professional or family responses that are either characterized by minimization or overreaction.

COMMON MYTHOLOGY AND MISINFORMATION

Roots and Early History of the Mythology. A myth, as defined in *Webster's Ninth New Collegiate Dictionary* (1986), is "a usually traditional story of ostensibly historical events that serves to unfold part of the worldview of a people or explain a practice, belief, or natu-

---

*Names and identifying characteristics in all case examples have been disguised thoroughly to protect privacy.

ral phenomenon" (p. 785). *Webster's* defines folklore as "a widely held unsupported notion or body of notions" (p. 479). How did we get to the point where much of our prevailing knowledge or understanding of firesetting behavior is saturated with myth and folklore? Surprisingly, the answer seems to be quite simple. Let's take a look back.

Firesetting and descriptions of specific punishments for the behavior have been present almost since the first time that man began to record history. Legal texts from the ancient Romans defined penalties for arson. In medieval England, convicted arsonists were assessed one hand and one foot and were banished from the country. Under 18th century French law, the crime of arson was punishable by death by hanging, decapitation, or quite ironically, burning at the stake (Steinbach, 1986).

In the early 1800s, attempts to explain, and not just exact punishments for, problematic firesetting behavior began to appear in French and German literature. Numerous German writers, most of whom were men of a very privileged class, presented an argument that firesetting behavior was predominantly to be found within the population of pubescent females who were of lowered cognitive functioning and who were experiencing menstrual difficulties. The firesetting behavior of these young women, it was theorized, was related to their abnormal psychosexual development (N. Lewis & Yarnell, 1951; Ray, 1838).

The term "pyromania" originated in France in the 1833 writings of a man named Marc who made the argument that pathological firesetters were suffering from a specific mental illness he termed "monomanie incendiare." For most of the 19th century, problematic firesetting was referred to in the literature as "Pyromania of Marc." For the most part, references to the disorder were presented in the context of controversial legal debates over the use of pyromania as an insanity defense for arson behavior. In 1838, Isaac Ray became the first American writer who wrote of some men having "a morbid propensity to incendiarism." It was not until the 1844 edition of *A Treatise on the Medical Jurisprudence of Insanity* that Ray specifically mentions the term pyromania. In it he presents a supportive argument for the work of prior European authors that pyromania be viewed as "a distinct form of insanity, annulling responsibility for the acts to which it leads" (Ray, 1844).

For the next 50 years, a medical and legal debate ensued between those who believed in the mental disorder theory of firesetting and those who viewed it as a criminal behavior (Geller, 1992). It was not until the assassination of President Garfield in 1881 that the debate appears to have ended in the United States as the country seemingly lost a tolerance for the insanity defense, and the term pyromania all but disappeared from American literature for the next 40 years.

Firesetting in Psychiatric Literature. While some turn-of-the-century authors had made isolated references to pyromania, it was not until Wilhelm Stekel, in his 1924 book *Peculiarities of Behavior*, reintroduced the debate within the psychiatric community. Stekel's focus upon the "sexual root" of pyromania, which gained a strong amount of support, defined it as a developmental disorder caused by impeded or unfulfilled sexual development.

Probably the most influential article on firesetting was written in 1932 by Sigmund Freud. Freud, it appears, had made a passing reference to firesetting in his 1930 book, *Civilization and Its Discontents*, and had been challenged by two authors to whom he was responding. In his 1932 article entitled "The Acquisition of Power Over Fire," Freud presented the following premise of his theory on the roots of man's attraction to fire:

> Now I conjectured that in order to possess himself of fire it was necessary for man to renounce his homosexually tinged desire to extinguish it with a stream of urine. I think that this conjecture can be confirmed by the interpretation of the Greek myth of Prometheus, provided we bear in mind the distortions to be expected in the transition from fact to the content of a myth. (p. 405)

Within this article, Freud details the importance of the psychoanalytic interpretation of the mythological story of Prometheus the Titan, the one who stole fire from the gods in a hollow rod, a fennel stalk. Freud describes the process of reversal, the transformation of an object into its opposite, as a central practice in psychoanalytic interpretation and therefore his belief in its usefulness in this instance. One is led to the realization that it is the "fluid" in the rod and not the fire that was of most interpretive value to Freud.

While Freud never wrote again on his urethral-erotic theory of firesetting behavior, his one article, based largely upon his prominence and influence in the study of human behavior at the time, significantly influenced the thinking of psychoanalytically trained physicians for decades. A review of the medical literature for the decades of the 1930s to the 1970s reveals references to this one article in the overwhelming majority of articles and studies. So strong was the influence of this theoretical understanding that in 1979, included within the collection of materials used for fire service promotional exams for Connecticut fire service personnel, it was suggested to fire investigators that arson suspects be escorted to the bathroom because "urination is a psychological form of sexual gratification for the pyromaniac, and it is impossible for him to function in front of others" (Barracato, 1979, p. 4).

Helen Yarnell, a psychiatrist at Bellevue Hospital in New York, appears to have been the first researcher to look specifically at children's and adolescent's involvement in firesetting. She later coauthored a landmark study on pathological firesetting with N. Lewis. N. Lewis and Yarnell (1951) expressed a cautionary note relative to the use of the "irresistible impulse" explanation of firesetting, stating that "the term is a favorite one with reporters, detectives, psychiatrists, and the offenders who adopt it for themselves as an easy, non-incriminating explanation for their behavior" (p. 86). Although quite influential, this study did not seem to end the debate on the etiology of firesetting.

The *DSM-I* (APA, 1952) classified pyromania as an obsessive-compulsive reaction while the *DSM-II* (APA, 1968) eliminated the diagnostic category entirely. Its specific distinction as an impulse disorder gained support during the 1970s and pyromania returned to the *DSM-III* (APA, 1980) and the *DSM-III-R* (APA, 1987) under the heading of "Disorders of Impulse Not Elsewhere Classified." While several authors and prominent researchers in the field openly question the integrity, and even the existence of the diagnosis of pyromania as it is presented in the literature (Geller, McDermeit, & Brown, 1997; Kolko, 1989), it remains included in the current *DSM-IV* (APA, 1994).

The diagnosis of pyromania, along with kleptomania and intermittent explosive disorder, comprise the *DSM-IV* category of Impulse Control Disorders Not Elsewhere Classified. The criteria for the application of a diagnosis of pyromania include:

1. Deliberate and purposeful firesetting on more than one occasion.
2. Tension or affective arousal before the act.
3. Fascination with, interest in, curiosity about, or attraction to fire and its situational contexts (e.g., paraphernalia, uses, consequences).
4. Pleasure, gratification, or relief when setting fires, or witnessing or participating in their aftermath.
5. The firesetting is not done for monetary gain, to express sociopolitical ideology, to conceal criminal activity, to express anger or vengeance, to improve one's living situation, to respond to a delusion or hallucination, or as a result of impaired

judgment (e.g., in dementia, Mental Retardation, Substance Intoxication).

6. The firesetting is not better accounted for by Conduct Disorder, a Manic Episode, or Antisocial Personality Disorder.

The Mythology of Firesetting. The confusion and lack of consensus in the medical, legal, sociological, and psychiatric literature have contributed significantly to the development and continued existence of a number of powerful "myths" regarding juveniles who engage in firesetting. Some of the more common myths are listed in Table 1 below.

TABLE 1: COMMON MYTHS RELATED TO JUVENILE FIRESETTING BEHAVIOR

- Juveniles who set fires are pyromaniacs or arsonists.
- Firesetting is related to enuresis.
- Firesetting is related to sexual deviancy and/or histories of sexual trauma.
- Firesetters are sexually aroused by their behavior.
- Juveniles who play with fire, or set fires, do so because of some "urge" or "obsession" with fire.
- Firesetting is related to cruelty to animals.
- Firesetting is a rare and isolated behavior that occurs among a small group of juveniles.
- Firesetters share a core set of deviant personality characteristics.
- Older children light more dangerous and deadly fires.
- Juveniles who display firesetting behaviors are likely to become adult firesetters.
- Firesetting is a difficult behavior to treat.
- Firesetting is more common among juveniles with lower intelligence levels.
- A therapy that allows juveniles to talk about their firesetting behavior will reduce their likelihood of firesetting.
- Playing with fire is part of a normal developmental phase for young children.
- Giving juveniles information about fire will encourage them to want to play with fire.

In regards to this prevailing mythology, it is perhaps Fineman (1995) who said it best:

The model that all firesetters are sexually repressed or obsessed, active or latent homosexual, enuretic, cruel to animals, and of subnormal intelligence must give way to a model that more accurately reflects the literature as well as the clinical impressions of those clinicians and fire service professionals who frequently evaluate firesetters. (p. 33)

FIRESETTING INCIDENCE
AND PREVALENCE DATA

Where then does this objective incidence and prevalence data exist? To what body of literature does one refer in order to begin gathering accurate and detailed information regarding the scope of the juvenile firesetting problem that we face in this country? The answer is surprisingly simple and quite alarming. The truth is that when it comes to juveniles and fire in the United States, we have on our hands a child and adolescent crisis of tremendous proportions. What is equally alarming is that many adults, professionals included, are simply unaware of the magnitude and complexity of the problem. It is contained in literature from the criminal justice, medical, fire service, educational, and mental health disciplines. During the past two decades, significant statistical evidence compiled by mental health, fire service, juvenile justice, and medical professionals consistently highlights the dramatic incidence rates for juvenile firesetting behavior in the United States.

Public Safety Data. Every year the misuse of fire by juveniles results in an almost unimaginable amount of physical and emotional damage. One can get a sense of the scope of the problem by reviewing the following data:

1. In 1997, public fire departments in the United States responded to over 1.7 million fires, an average of one fire every 18 seconds (National Fire Protection Association [NFPA], 1997).
2. Eighty percent of all fire deaths occur in the home (Hall, 1997).
3. In the United States, juveniles are responsible for *over 40%* of all structure fires (Snyder, 1998).
4. Burn injuries are the second leading cause of accidental death for children under the age of 6 (Federal Emergency Management Agency [FEMA], 1988).
5. A significant percentage, estimated between 40% to 50%, of children and adolescents admitted to medical units for treatment of burns, are burned in fires set by themselves or another child or adolescent (Barth, 1988; Jayaprakash, Jung, & Panitch, 1984).
6. A 1994 survey conducted by the Children's Hospital Burn Center in Colorado concluded that more than 78% of juveniles treated for flame burn injuries were burned in juvenile-set fires (Children's Hospital Burn Center, 1997).
7. Nearly 40% of all fire-related deaths involve children under the age of 5. This is a rate that is more than double the rate for any other age group (Hall, 1997).

8. In 1993, 76% of the 408 deaths due to juvenile-set fires were preschool-aged children who were most likely to be found in their own bedrooms (Hall, 1995).
9. Younger children set the most dangerous fires in regards to fatalities and injuries while older children set fires that generally result in greater dollar loss (NFPA, 1997).
10. Among 5- to 14-year-olds, fires and burns rank third among causes of death (National Center for Health Statistics, 1984).

Sadly, the majority of the thousands of children killed or injured in house fires each year are killed or injured in fires set by themselves or another child (FEMA, 1988). Over the past 25 years, with the advent of smoke detector and sprinkler system legislation, the residential fire death rates for all age groups have been dramatically reduced — with one exception. Our youngest and most helpless children, those under the age of 6, are significantly more likely to die in a house fire than any other age group. In fact, 39% of all fire deaths involve children under the age of 5 (Hall, 1997).

Every day our hospital wards care for victims of our juvenile firesetting problem. This is especially true of those units and hospitals dedicated solely to the care of burn victims. The Shriners, one of the largest and most active fraternal organizations in the world, remain dedicated to raising money to provide free medical care to pediatric burn victims. Each year hundreds of millions of dollars are raised to be spent on the medical care of juveniles whose burn scars will never heal, whose physical disfigurement is sometimes grotesque, and whose emotional damage is often the greatest price paid.

Criminal Justice Data. Our juvenile firesetting problem extends far beyond our own homes and hospital wards. Across the country our middle schools and high schools, vacant buildings, dumpsters, churches, and wooded areas fall victim daily to fires set accidentally or intentionally by children and adolescents. The overwhelming majority of school fires occur during the school day when buildings are filled with students and teachers. School bathrooms, trash barrels, and lockers are frequently reported in the cause and origin reports filed by local fire departments. Yet statistics are only gathered for those fires that are reported to the fire department and do not include the many fires that are extinguished by school personnel and not reported for fear of the public's reaction.

The FBI defines arson as "any willful or malicious burning or attempt to burn, with or without intent to defraud, a dwelling house, public building, motor vehicle or aircraft, personal property of another, etc." (Snyder, 1998). While hundreds of millions of dollars are being spent each year to address the growing problem of youth violence in our country, precious little is being specifically and systematically directed towards the largest juvenile crime problem in our country — *arson*. A review of our criminal justice statistics reveals

1. Over 50% of all arrests for arson in the United States involve children under the age of 18 (Snyder, 1998).
2. More juveniles are arrested for arson than for any other violent crime tracked by the FBI. From 1986 to 1995 the juvenile arrest rate for arson rose by 40% (Snyder, 1998).
3. Of those juveniles arrested for arson, 33% were under the age of 15 (Alexander, 1997).
4. In the state of Oregon, arson arrests for juveniles rose 66% from 1990 to 1994 (Oregon State Fire Marshal, 1996).
5. Fifty-five percent of all school building arson fires were committed by juveniles (Alexander, 1997).

Despite these startling statistics, some fire service and criminal justice professionals are quick to point out that juvenile arson rates could even be higher because in nearly 80% to 85% of cases involving "suspicious" fires the offender is never determined. Yet how many intelligent adults would know that arson is the number one violent juvenile crime in the United States? How many would even realize it is one of the top three violent crimes committed by children and adolescents?

Property Loss Data. The final cost of the juvenile firesetting problem in our country is quite literally a financial one. As a nation we are losing millions of dollars per day to this problem in construction costs alone. Data kept at the state and local levels reveal similar patterns and levels of losses. These figures do not even take into account the costs to communities to extinguish these fires, provide temporary housing, lost wages, and the medical costs for injuries sustained by firefighters and civilians. Yet the data are startling:

1. Between 1992 and 1996, residential and commercial structure fires in the United States resulted in the loss of *over $4.6 billion* in property damage and those fires which were known to be juvenile-set fires accounted for over $240 million of that loss (NFPA, 1998).

2. School fires account for over $200 million annually in property loss. More than half of these fires are set intentionally, and over 75% of them occur during the school day (NFPA, 1997).
3. From 1992 to 1994 the state of Oregon reported a doubling of the dollar loss figure to over $2 million from juveniles playing with fire (Oregon State Fire Marshal, 1996).
4. Fires started by juveniles in Phoenix, Arizona, in 1 year resulted in a loss exceeding $1.1 million (Phoenix Fire Department, 1999).
5. In 1997, the 121 cleared child arson cases in Houston, Texas, which include only those cases in which a child was apprehended and prosecuted, had resulted in the loss of $2,437,725 in property (Houston Fire Department, 1998).

Considering the incidence and prevalence data made available during the past decade, it is dramatically evident that the size and scope of the juvenile firesetting problem is of incredible magnitude and involves great numbers of juveniles. Why are so many children and adolescents involved in this dangerous and destructive behavior? Who are these children and adolescents? What are their characteristics? Prior to exploring the more common motivational profiles of juveniles who become involved in firesetting, there are some fundamental demographic and diagnostic data that have crystallized over the past decade that merit mentioning.

Gender. Firesetting behavior is, and always has been, predominantly a male behavior. It is commonly reported that boys are responsible for 75% to 85% of all firesetting behavior, with increasing percentages of females present in the 13- to 17-year-old group (Kolko, 1985; Saunders & Awad, 1991). Some authors have reported over 30% involvement by females at these older ages (Porth, 1997). There is very little research data that is available that explores any differences that might be present between female firesetters and their male counterparts.

Age. Children and adolescents of all ages engage in fireplay and firesetting behaviors. Some programs and studies have reported firesetting involvement by children as young as 2 years. Several studies have looked at age as a variable in relation to firesetting behavior and appear to have arrived at similar conclusions (Grolnick et al., 1990; Kolko, 1985). While the average age for firesetting is around 10, a meaningless statistic if there ever was one, there appear to be several key developmental points at which increased levels of firesetting behavior are evident. Children between the ages of 3 and 5, or mid- to late-toddlerhood, are overrepresented in much of the statistical data. One would speculate that this is impacted by several developmental variables including an increased level of cognitive curiosity of their environment, the development of the fine motor skills necessary to strike a match or engage a lighter, and increasing struggles with parents around limit setting and behaviors.

In addition, early adolescents (ages 12-15) appear to be overrepresented in the program and research data. Again, one could assume that developmental issues such as increased experimental behaviors, the growing importance of peer relationships, and increased need to gain independence through defying authority figures (parents, teachers) are closely related to this phenomenon. Despite these patterns, it is important for practitioners to remember that firesetting can, and does, happen at any age.

Parent and Family Characteristics. There is an emerging body of evidence (Fineman, 1995; Gale, 1999; Gruber, Heck, & Mintzer, 1981; Kazdin & Kolko, 1986; Kolko & Kazdin, 1990; Reis, 1993; Sakheim & Osborn, 1994) which indicates that the parents and families of children and adolescents engaged in firesetting, when compared to nonfiresetting families, display a set of behavioral, emotional, and parenting style characteristics that include the following:

1. Maximum amounts of internal stress combined with minimal problem-solving abilities.
2. Decreased levels of structure, monitoring, and rule enforcement in the home.
3. Increased reports of depression among mothers of firesetting children and adolescents.
4. Decreased levels of affective expression.
5. Higher levels of personal and marital distress, parenting difficulties, and family dysfunction.
6. Lower levels of agreement with partners resulting in greater parent discord.
7. Parents report higher levels of having had their own history of significant problems including domestic violence, mental illness, and substance abuse.

Clinical Incidence and Prevalence. Despite the relatively small amount of research data available, there are studies that suggest that prevalence rates for juvenile firesetting might be higher than most people think. Among children and adolescents receiving outpatient mental health services, firesetting appears among roughly 15% to 20% of patients (Heath et al., 1985; Kolko & Kazdin, 1988; Showers & Pickrell, 1987) with even higher rates (25%-40%) found among inpatient and delinquent populations (Hanson et al., 1994; Kolko & Kazdin, 1988).

Diagnostic Classification. While it is commonly held that the population of children and adolescents involved in firesetting behavior are a heterogeneous group and that the setting of a fire separate from all other factors means little diagnostically, the growing body of literature points to the prominence of several diagnostic categories among the firesetting population (Gale, 1999; Heath et al., 1985; Kolko & Kazdin, 1988; Kuhnley, Hendren, & Quinland, 1982; Moore, Thompson-Pope, & Whited, 1996; Showers & Pickrell, 1987).

The diagnostic entities included in the Attention-Deficit and Disruptive Behavior Disorders category of the *DSM-IV* (APA, 1994) are significantly overrepresented in the population of firesetting children and adolescents. Children and adolescents who meet the diagnostic criteria of (a) Attention-Deficit/Hyperactivity Disorders (ADHD), (b) Conduct Disorder, (c) Oppositional Defiant Disorder, and (d) Disruptive Behavior Disorder NOS are more commonly seen among the population of children and adolescents involved in community programs, outpatient clinic programs, residential treatment programs, detention and correctional facilities, and hospital-based programs that address firesetting.

While these four diagnostic categories are most prominent, it is important for practitioners to remember that some of the children and adolescents involved in firesetting do not meet any diagnostic criteria while others display very complex and serious diagnostic profiles. It is the heterogeneity of this population that makes the issue of assessment so critical and the work so fascinating. Clinicians are likely to encounter children and adolescents whose diagnostic profiles range from more benign adjustment disorders to the most severe character and personality disorders. If asked what kinds of children are likely to set a fire, mental health professionals who have worked extensively with firesetting behavior would most likely respond

- Children who have access to lighters and matches set fires.
- Children who have little fire knowledge set fires.
- Children who are curious set fires.
- Children who are impulsive set fires.
- Children who are nonverbal/performance learners set fires.
- Children who are mischievous and oppositional set fires.

- Children who have learning disabilities set fires.
- Children who have been physically or sexually abused set fires.
- Children who are anxious and traumatized set fires.
- Children who are socially awkward and isolated set fires.
- Children who are sad and depressed set fires.
- Children who find it hard to communicate with words set fires.
- Children who are angry and hostile set fires.
- Children who feel rejected and abandoned set fires.
- Children who are thrill seeking set fires.
- Children who are violent and aggressive set fires.
- Children who have a serious mental illness set fires.

Pyromania, Sex, and Firesetting. The earliest and most influential theories on the etiology of firesetting — those that described either sexual or impulsive roots — have received attention by several researchers who have looked to clarify or identify their existence in various patient populations (Geller, 1992; Harris & Rice, 1996; Kolko, 1989). There appears to be a strong consensus among most of their findings that the evidence for sexual motivations for firesetting are based largely upon anecdotal references and literary analyses and not on the findings of controlled studies. In a study that involved the administration of penile tumenscence measures to adult firesetters and nonfiresetters, researchers found no differences in sexual responses to images of fire that were presented to research subjects (Quinsey, Chaplin, & Upfold, 1989).

Those studies that have explored incidence rates for pyromania have continually reported that even among the most disturbed population of adults — those who will spend large portions of their lives in secure treatment facilities and have chronic histories of pathological and dangerous firesetting — the existence of pyromania is quite rare. In fact, the clinical and experimental data provide very little support for the diagnostic integrity of the disorder. If this is true, then the likelihood of coming across a child or an adolescent who meets the criteria for this controversial diagnosis is infinitesimal.

FIRESETTING THEORY

Over the past 20 years there has been a small but concerted effort among several professionals to articulate a comprehensive and structured model to help practitioners identify and conceptualize those variables which contribute to the likelihood that a juvenile will become involved in firesetting. Despite these efforts, firesetting remains best understood as an often complex behavior that is mediated by several intervening variables which may prove to be resistant to theoretical efforts to simplify and categorize it.

Dynamic-Behavioral Formulation. The earliest effort to define a conceptual, social-psychological framework of factors related to juvenile firesetting occurred in the early 1980s and was led in part by Dr. Kenneth Fineman (Fineman, 1980). Since the early development of Fineman's "dynamic-behavioral" theory of firesetting, other authors have further articulated the theory's applicability to firesetting behavior (Cook et al., 1989; Gaynor, 1991). It was also the impetus for the development of three assessment instruments to help evaluators understand the sequence of thought, behavior, and affect that accompanies firesetting behavior in children, adolescents, and adults (Fineman, 1995).

The dynamic-behavioral theory presents a model that helps identify a set of factors related to the (a) personality and individual characteristics, (b) family and social circumstances, and (c) immediate environmental conditions which are believed to set the stage for firesetting behavior. It views firesetting behavior as an interaction between dynamic historical factors that predispose the firesetter toward a variety of maladaptive and antisocial acts, historical environmental factors that have taught and reinforced firesetting as acceptable, and immediate environmental contingencies that encourage firesetting behavior. From its inception, the author has held that the value of the model is its role in the development of a quantitative measure of various independent variables (i.e., personality, social, environmental) that will predict the occurrence of the dependent variable (firesetting). In 1995, Dr. Fineman presented his quantitative analysis model for measuring risk for firesetting, which is described briefly in the review of assessment models and protocols.

Social-Learning Model. Later in the 1980s, researchers David Kolko and Alan Kazdin (1986) presented their conceptualization of a social-learning model of firesetting behavior as a "tentative" risk factor model. Kolko and Kazdin highlighted the fact that firesetting is truly a multidisciplinary problem, involving professionals from mental health, fire service, juvenile justice, and community organizations. In addition, they emphasize that the absence of one central focus has significantly hindered the task of integrating research findings and determining research directions — a problem that continues to exist today.

The social-learning model highlights several factors believed to be related to firesetting within three domains:

1. Learning experiences and cues.
2. Personal repertoire.
3. Parent and family influences and stressors.

Kolko and Kazdin presented the outline in Table 2 (below) to provide a more detailed description of the items that comprise each of the three domains.

TABLE 2: SOCIAL-LEARNING MODEL FOR FIRESETTING BEHAVIOR CONCEPTUAL SYNTHESIS: A TENTATIVE RISK MODEL*

---

1. Learning Experiences and Cues

   a. Early modeling (vicarious) experiences
   b. Early interest and direct experiences
   c. Availability of adult models and incendiary materials

2. Personal Repertoire

   a. Cognitive Components

      • Limited fire-awareness and fire safety skills

   b. Behavioral Components

      • Interpersonal ineffectiveness/skills deficits
      • Antisocial behavior excesses

   c. Motivational Components

3. Parent and Family Influences and Stressors

   a. Limited supervision and monitoring
   b. Parental distance and uninvolvement
   c. Parental pathology and limitations
   d. Stressful external events

---

*Note. From "A Conceptualization of Firesetting in Children and Adolescents," by D. Kolko and A. Kazdin, 1986, *Journal of Abnormal Child Psychology, 14*(1), p. 51. Copyright © 1986 by Kluwer Academic/Plenum Publishers. Reprinted with permission.

Cycles of Firesetting: An Oregon Model. The Oregon Treatment Strategies Task Force and the Office of the Oregon State Fire Marshal have developed the Cycles Model of Firesetting based upon the clinical experience of members of the task force and designed to provide a framework for discussing a juvenile's firesetting behavior (Oregon Treatment Strategies Task Force, 1996). The Cycles Model is visually represented by four concentric and interrelated circles that represent the four dimensions of a juvenile's internal and external world that are considered to be related to their likelihood of firesetting.

The "emotional/cognitive cycle," represented by the innermost circle, focuses upon the variety of thoughts and feelings that juveniles may experience after their fire involvement. The "behavior cycle," the next innermost circle, concerns the actual behaviors and actions of the juvenile and their relationship to the thoughts and feelings identified earlier. The family's response to the firesetting behavior and the over-all emotional environment of the family are critical variables that are represented in the "family/household" cycle. Finally, the "community/social" cycle addresses groups outside the family and the level of support or restriction that impacts the juvenile and the family.

MOTIVATIONAL TYPOLOGIES

One of the critical variables which has been the focus of much research and literature attention is the attempt to articulate and catego-rize, in an understandable and simplified format, a child's or an adolescent's motivation for his or her firesetting behavior (Fineman, 1980, 1995; Gaynor & Hatcher, 1987; Kolko & Kazdin, 1991b; Swaffer & Hollin, 1995; Vreeland & Waller, 1979; Wooden & Berkey, 1984). While any individual variable by itself is limited, motivation remains the most popular, and relatively simplest, method by which practition-ers and researchers have been attempting to place children and adoles-cents who have been involved with firesetting into structured types, typologies, or profiles.

At the present time these motivational categories are best under-stood as guidelines or frameworks to aid the mental health profes-sional in formulating an understanding of a juvenile's firesetting be-haviors and not as diagnostic or descriptive categories. Indeed many children and adolescents will present with multiple, and often extremely complex, motivations that limit the ability of practitioners to assign them within the simplified models that currently exist.

"Curiosity" Motivated Firesetting. These are the stories that lead the evening news — a house fire typically set in the early morning or late afternoon which kills one or more young children whose bodies are found hidden in a closet or under the bed in their bedroom. More often than not, the trailing remarks of the reporter, lost in the graphic images of flame and smoke, mention that it is believed the fire was started as a result of a child "playing with matches."

"Curiosity," by simple definition, is the "desire to know." It is commonly accepted among most adults that a child's curiosity about fire, especially at certain developmental levels, is perfectly normal

(Bumpass, Fagelman, & Brix, 1983; Grolnick et al., 1990; Hanson et al., 1995). While the term "curiosity firesetting" is used in this book, the same behavior has been described in other writings as "playing with matches," "nonpathological firesetting," or "fireplay."

Curiosity firesetting, the most commonly reported motivation for firesetting behavior, is driven by a child's desire to learn about or master fire through actual experimentation or play. These are the children and adolescents who are attempting to learn about fire through actual handling and manipulation: playing with matches or lighters; candle play; watching small pieces of paper burn; burning small plastic toys or food items to "see what happens to them"; or throwing small objects (matchbox cars, insects) into fireplaces, campfires, or barbecue pits. As a characteristic of personal temperament, the amount of curiosity displayed by individual children and adolescents falls along a continuum. Many children and adolescents are highly curious about everything in their environment, and their curiosity about fire is naturally higher than that of children and adolescents whose temperaments are less curious by nature. These highly curious children are often described as being "fascinated" or "obsessed" with fire.

Efforts to describe curiosity motivated firesetting, as with all of the other motivational typologies that have been defined, include descriptive information about the children and adolescents themselves, parental and family environment characteristics, and characteristics of the fires which they set (Fineman, 1995; Kolko & Kazdin, 1991b; Pinsonneault & Richardson, 1989a). While the descriptive information presented in Table 3 (p. 22) is reflective of current knowledge, it is important to note that curiosity firesetting can happen at any time, in any family, by any child, of any age.

At first glance one might think that these young, curious children who are lighting fires with ordinary materials would present as the least dangerous. The truth is that it is exactly these children who are setting the most deadly fires when compared to other age groups. The combination of hidden fire locations, poor adult supervision, lack of working smoke detectors, and children who often do not understand the danger of fire growth sets the stage for a fire's ability to get a 2- to 3-minute head start before discovery. Given this head start, these fires typically result in a tremendous amount of property damage and, tragically, the loss of young lives. While the motives of these young children, as compared to those of older children, are often simple, the sad reality is that a higher percentage of their fires result in fatalities and serious burn injury.

TABLE 3: "CURIOSITY" MOTIVATED FIRESETTING

A. Characteristics of the Children/Adolescents

- Tend to be younger (ages 3-7).
- About 90% are boys.
- Higher rates of impulsivity (ADHD) and ability to resist/defy authority.
- Often described as "into everything," "hard to control," "adventurous," "mischievous," and "aggressive."
- Often are performance (nonverbal) learners. They learn by touching, experimenting, and manipulating, not by asking.
- Younger children are more concrete learners and therefore lack an understanding of the capacity of fire to grow rapidly.
- Early risers, frequently seeking stimulation (physical activity, video games).
- Lack an understanding or appreciation of the dangerousness of fire.
- Often are remorseful about the behavior.

B. Characteristics of the Parent/Family Environment

- Environment provides ready access to lighters and matches.
- Often one or both parents smoke.
- Periods of poor supervision by adults (often a single-parent household).
- Parents often have limited parenting abilities to manage the difficult behaviors of their children. Rely predominantly on punishment instead of instruction.
- Limited understanding of normal child development results in negative, counterproductive responses to child's normal curiosity.
- Parents have limited fire safety awareness and homes are poorly prepared for fire (e.g., smoke detectors, extinguishers, escape plans).

C. Characteristics of the Fires

- Fires are set in the home or within close proximity (i.e., backyard).
- Often set in hidden locations such as a closet or under a bed.
- Fires are often set early in the morning or during afterschool hours.
- Ordinary ignition sources (matches and lighters) and ordinary combustibles (paper, toys, food).
- Many of these children have single episodes of firesetting, while others engage in an identifiable pattern of fire exploration.
- In some cases they will escalate to involve the use of stove, fireplace, toasters, or baseboard heating elements as a heat source.

"Crisis" Motivated Firesetting. Throughout all of the literature on juvenile firesetting, there is clear agreement that many children and adolescents use fire, either consciously or unconsciously, as a means of communicating their distress or in an effort to seek relief from their distress (Fineman, 1995; Kafry, 1980; Kolko & Kazdin, 1991b; Swaffer & Hollin, 1995; Wooden & Berkey, 1984). They have also been referred to in the literature as the "cry for help," "pathological," "troubled," or "angry" firesetter. Very often these juveniles are described as being ineffective, anxious, and seemingly powerless in their world, a world that they often experience as being out of their control. Understandably, a child who struggles with attempting to verbally express his feelings and thoughts to others would be drawn to the most powerful element in the universe to do the talking for them. Why struggle to find the appropriate words to express your sense of abandonment and rejection by your father when taking a match to his favorite shirt or CD collection can speak volumes?

The other powerful attraction to fire for these children and adolescents is the sense of mastery and competence that they may feel as they engage in their fire behaviors as compared to the struggles they have in their friendships, schools, or families. For them the "crisis" is an internal one as they are frequently described as being ineffective, anxious, or awkward. Let's face it, if you can master or control one of the most powerful elements in the universe, then everything else would pale in comparison. Imagine the immediate sense of importance an overweight, learning disabled 12-year-old boy can feel as he pours butane into his cupped hand, ignites it, and proudly shows it to all of the 14- to 15-year-olds who stand in awe. When he adds the proclamation, "I'm the fire guy!", his sense of identity and importance in his peer group, the only group he has real membership in, has increased exponentially.

The information presented in Table 4 (p. 24) represents characteristics that are typical of "crisis" motivated children, their fires, and their families.

The large majority of juveniles who have engaged in crisis motivated firesetting are juveniles with whom we, as mental health professionals, are quite familiar. They are the very same children and adolescents who frequent our clinic offices, school counseling centers, court clinics, residential facilities, and psychiatric hospitals.

"Delinquent" Motivated Firesetting. Our juvenile firesetting problem moves well beyond our homes and backyards. The use of fire as a means of acting out against authority is a daily occurrence in this country. More often than not these fires are characterized by the fact that they are set outside the home and involve the actions and decision making of two or more children or adolescents. They are the result of combinations of negative peer influences, poor decision-making abilities, wishes to impress or fit in, and tendencies to act in ways that violate social norms.

Within this category are juveniles of great variety and levels of delinquent personality traits and behavior. At one end of the continuum

---

TABLE 4: "CRISIS" MOTIVATED FIRESETTING

A. Characteristics of the Children/Adolescents

- Predominantly boys (75%-85%).
- Most commonly fall within latency and early adolescent range (6-12 years old).
- May or may not have a history of prior fire involvement or interest.
- Often described as ineffective, socially awkward, or powerless.
- Histories of physical, sexual, or emotional abuse.
- Poor verbal communicators of their thoughts and feelings.
- Diagnostically heterogeneous group — may include a range of children from those with no prior mental health history to children who are seriously emotionally disturbed.
- Experience higher rates of social/friendship problems. Often described as loners, socially unassertive, or as having chronic conflicts with peers.
- Appear to display little remorse for the fire behavior or understanding of the potential impact upon others.

B. Characteristics of the Parent/Family Environment

- Varied demographic and socioeconomic backgrounds.
- Identified crisis or stressor(s) in the family that may include a physically or emotionally abusive environment, the death of a close relative, separation or divorce of parents, drug or alcohol abuse, domestic violence, loss of job, relocation, or death of a pet.
- Family responds poorly to the crisis or stressor. Unable to provide resolution and emotional support for child.
- Crisis can take the form of single, acute episode or be a more chronic condition within the family.
- Themes of power and control play a prominent role.
- Often are resistant to intervention and change.

C. Characteristics of the Fires

- Often the fires set by these children are highly symbolic or communicative (i.e., they tell a story).
- Timing, location, sequence of fire activity, or target of the fire (bed, clothing, personal property) can be significant factors.
- Child may use a "favorite lighter" as ignition source.
- Rarely are the fires designed to hurt others.

---

are juveniles who engage in a single episode of high risk and socially unacceptable fire behavior to gain social acceptance within their peer group. The 13-year-old social outcast who suddenly has the opportunity to be "one of the guys" by participating in the lighting of a dumpster in the neighborhood or toilet paper rolls in the school bathroom makes a poor decision with little intent to harm others. At the other end of the continuum are those juveniles whose firesetting behavior reflects a personality structure and set of cognitive beliefs that completely disregards the safety of others. Their firesetting is part of a chronic and pervasive pattern of criminal behavior and includes fires that are intentionally set to destroy property, injure, or threaten and control others. Kolko and Kazdin (1986) propose that firesetting within this adolescent population is frequently a manifestation of both anxiety and anger and is therefore a more complex level of antisocial behavior than mere Conduct Disorder.

During the past decade, delinquent juvenile firesetting behavior has received relatively little research attention and resources as compared to the other violent crimes committed by juveniles. While somewhat limited in sample size and scope of study, the studies and surveys that have been completed have provided increasing amounts of descriptive data on the characteristics of these juveniles, their families, and the fires which they set (Forehand et al., 1991; Gale, 1999; Hanson et al., 1994; Moore et al., 1996; Reis, 1993; Sakheim, Osborn, & Abrams, 1991). Table 5 (p. 26) summarizes those characteristics.

"Pathologically" Motivated Firesetting. While the image of the bizarre and deviant individual as the arsonist or pyromaniac is one of the most common portrayals in the media, as well as in the mental health literature, it is fortunately the rarest of the motivations seen by professionals working in the field (Rice & Harris, 1991). This group of severely disturbed children and adolescents includes those who are actively psychotic, acutely paranoid or delusional, or children and adolescents who have lived in chronically disturbed and bizarre environments. Within this relatively rare group of juveniles is a subgroup who is motivated sufficiently by the internal sensory reinforcement (sight, sound, smell) of fire (Fineman, 1995). If the degree of sensory reinforcement is powerful enough, then consideration of a diagnosis of Pyromania must be given. Not all pathologically motivated firesetters meet the criteria for pyromania. In fact most will not. They are, however, to be included in the larger category of juveniles who are pathologically motivated to set fires.

These juveniles and their families have most often demonstrated significant deficits in functioning for long periods of time in home environments characterized by deprivation and neglect, physical and sexual abuse, parent drug and alcohol abuse, and domestic violence. As a result of the damage that these factors wreak on them, these children and adolescents display neurological, cognitive, and emotional deficits that are strikingly evident and most often permanent.

Several years ago I had the opportunity to interview, at a locked state hospital unit, a 15-year-old girl who had been implicated in the

TABLE 5: "DELINQUENT" MOTIVATED FIRESETTING

A.   Characteristics of the Children/Adolescents

  • Older children and adolescents (10-17 years old).
  • While still predominantly a male behavior, within this group you will see higher percentages of female involvement (25%-30%) than for curiosity, crisis, or pathological motivated firesetting populations.
  • Poorly developed social and interpersonal skills.
  • Significant proportion of juveniles who meet criteria for Oppositional Defiant Disorder or Conduct Disorder.
  • When compared to their nonfiresetting delinquent peers, they are often identified as displaying a more "high trajectory" form of Conduct Disorder characterized by early onset and rapid escalation of criminal and antisocial behaviors.
  • Histories of school failure and behavioral problems.
  • Limited recognition or appreciation of danger to self and others that their firesetting behaviors create. Little precaution taken to prevent injury to themselves or others.
  • Often display chronic histories of maltreatment and abuse.

B.   Characteristics of the Parent/Family Environment

  • Parents have high rates of substance abuse, domestic violence, involvement with the law, and social instability.
  • Parenting styles tend be highly rigid and punitive in nature but often are inconsistent in the administration of consequences.
  • Parents are highly resistant or directly confrontational with service providers.
  • Ability to provide a safe environment for their children is significantly compromised.
  • Limited understanding of child development and have responded quite negatively to their children's efforts to be more independent.

C.   Characteristics of the Fires

  • Fires are most often set outside the home. Locations include schools, vacant buildings, dumpsters, wooded areas, and abandoned vehicles.
  • Includes fires set for purposes of vandalism to public property or fires set to target the property of a specific individual.
  • Delinquent fires can also result from ongoing group dynamics and include motivation more related to efforts to impress other group members or to "fit in" with a peer group.
  • Fires involve increased use of dangerous chemical accelerants (gasoline, aerosol sprays) and other explosive materials in a highly irresponsible manner (games, challenges).
  • Decisions to set a fire are often the result of group thinking and influence.

arson fire of her neighbor's home. During the interview she was quite willing to admit that she had deliberately set her neighbor's house on fire because the man who owned the home had treated her disrespectfully the day before and that she had taken great care to conceal her criminal actions, albeit unsuccessfully. In order to avoid her neighbor's motion-sensitive spotlights, she had sneaked into his yard during daylight hours and constructed a trail of dry leaves from her yard to the woodpile that was attached to his home. She had then poured a small amount of gasoline along the 25-foot trail of leaves. At around 2 a.m. she awoke and climbed out of her bedroom window to the backyard, ignited the pile of leaves, immediately returned to her room, and closed her window and shade to "watch the glow." She later went outside to watch the firefighters and all the people crying.

A review of her records revealed a young lady who had been subjected to incredible physical and sexual abuse, had lived with an uncle who had been implicated in numerous aggressive firesetting incidents and with whom she would spend nights listening to the police/fire scanner, had experienced the loss of any substantial relationship with her mother who had been severely head injured in a fall, had been violently raped on at least two occasions, and whose cognitive functioning had last been measured as being in the moderately deficient range.

Nearing the end of our final interview in the hospital, she leaned over the table and whispered in a secretive manner, "The rest of my fires are downstairs." When asked what she meant, she reported that she had her "fire diary" hidden in her trunk of belongings in the basement of the hospital. Allowed to retrieve it, she opened to a meticulously kept record of the date, time, and location of every fire she had ever set. There were 374 entries. She went on to describe in great detail the ritual-like process of always burning only five sticks, in one of three safe locations in the woods, and watching the colors and flames "dance" for 5 to 10 minutes which "made me feel gooder."

The literature of pathological or severely disturbed firesetting supports the following descriptive information that might serve to distinguish it from other forms of firesetting (see Table 6, p. 28).

SOLVING THE ASSESSMENT PUZZLE

FIRESETTING ASSESSMENT ISSUES

Juvenile firesetting is a perplexing, dangerous, and fascinating behavior that often results from the influence of a complex set of internal and external factors related to the child or adolescent, the characteristics of their environment, or the occurrence of a specific precipitating event. The mental health professional's ability to accurately and

---

TABLE 6: "PATHOLOGICALLY" MOTIVATED FIRESETTING

A. Characteristics of the Children/Adolescents

- Typically adolescent age (13-17) with a majority being males.
- Chronic histories of multiple deficit areas (cognitive, neurological, emotional).
- Poor response to extensive prior interventions and support services.
- Often the presence of compromised and distorted thinking in the form of paranoia, hallucinations, or delusions.
- Abject deficits in problem solving, interpersonal relations, and social skills.
- Have been victimized in any number of ways (physical, sexual, emotional).
- Often have had histories of early fascination with fire that have developed through time as a coping mechanism or have been integrated as a part of their personality.

B. Characteristics of the Parent/Family Environment

- Chaotic, violent, and abusive homes.
- Parents display multiple deficits.
- Family history is often remarkable for major mental illnesses.

C. Characteristics of the Fires

- Numerous fires, often in the hundreds.
- Fires are lit in a solitary and secretive manner.
- Often the fires have a ritualistic and repetitive quality to them.
- Fires are often described in human qualities (dancing, soothing).

---

thoroughly analyze the cause or nature of a condition, situation, or problem is the product of both scientific process and artistic endeavor. Few would argue that it is the provision of an accurate diagnostic formulation that leads directly to the identification of appropriate and available treatment services which ultimately lead to relief from, or a reduction in the severity of, the identified problem. Assessment is at the very root of the therapeutic process.

Numerous authors have reported on the importance of a comprehensive diagnostic approach when a mental health professional attempts to provide to others an understanding of a child's or an adolescent's firesetting behavior (Fineman, 1995; Hanson et al., 1995; Kolko & Kazdin, 1989a; Sakheim & Osborn, 1994). As such, firesetting presents itself as a particularly robust challenge to mental health professionals who are attempting to gather relevant information in order to gain insight into, and develop an understanding of, a juvenile's firesetting behaviors. From this insight and understanding rises the opportunity to identify appropriate treatment recommendations. If, as a mental health professional, you are drawn to complex diagnostic processes, firesetting behavior will definitely be of interest to you.

A basic tenet of the diagnostic process is that every assessment, evaluation, or examination begins with questions or concerns about a particular problem and ultimately the search for a solution. These diagnostic questions, which serve to define the diagnostic process, are derived from the presenting symptoms — whether they be pains in one's chest, squeaking car brakes, firesetting behavior, or anything in between. After experiencing chest pain, one is likely to ask a cardiac physician, "What is this pain, and how worried do I need to be?" When you seek your mechanic's advice regarding the screeching sound your car engine has been making, you might ask, "What is this noise, and how worried do I need to be?" From this initial description of the symptoms, the physician and mechanic alike decide what steps, tools, and techniques will be required in order for them to gather enough information to provide you with an informed and accurate answer. Sometimes it is a relatively simple process and at other times it can be quite lengthy, complex, and even painful.

Clinician Background and Skills. Assessment of human behavior within the field of psychology remains a uniquely unavoidable combination of both art and science. The mental health professional who is interested in assessing firesetting behavior — a dangerous behavior that has the capacity to injure and victimize others — must develop a set of attitudes, acquire a base of fire-specific knowledge, and professionally practice a core set of interviewing and diagnostic skills. Professional and ethical guidelines clearly establish the responsibility of the individual to develop and maintain his or her professional competence (American Psychological Association, 1992).

Most similar to the field of the assessment and treatment of firesetting behavior is that of sex offending behavior which, when compared to firesetting, has a more organized network of professionals and greater body of literature that articulates necessary skills for working with the sex offending population of children and adolescents. Literature from professional groups working with sex offenders (W. Cormier & L. Cormier, 1985; Egan, 1990; Enfield, 1987; Perry & Orchard, 1992) provides a framework for the general and specific clinical skills that are seen as necessary prerequisites for the assessment and treatment of child and adolescent sex offenders. These skills appear to translate easily into guidelines for professionals who are interested in working with child and adolescent firesetters (see Table 7, p. 30).

TABLE 7:   SUGGESTED GUIDELINES FOR PROFESSIONALS WORKING WITH CHILD/ADOLESCENT FIRESETTERS

- Listening and empathy skills.
- Skills in confronting deception, distortion, or minimization.
- Ability to support the child/adolescent and maintain a working relationship.
- Solid base of knowledge in the area of psychological theory, diagnostics, and behavior measures.
- Solid base of content knowledge in the areas of fire science and behavior, fire safety knowledge, and burn care.
- Awareness of current knowledge about child and adolescent firesetting.
- Adequate training that includes a period of supervised clinical practice.
- Ability to work effectively within a multidisciplinary structure that involves active cooperation with fire service, law enforcement, social service, and education professionals.

FIRESETTING ASSESSMENT MODELS, PROTOCOLS, AND TOOLS

The diagnostic process for the clinical assessment of child or adolescent firesetting behavior — and the decision as to what steps, tools, and techniques will be necessary to complete an evaluation — typically begins with a request by a parent, a mental health professional, a social service agency, a residential care provider, or a representative from the juvenile justice system for answers to the following questions (Stadolnik, 1998a):

1. Why is this juvenile involved in firesetting behavior? How are we to understand its meaningfulness or the purpose it serves for them?
2. What level of fire knowledge and fire safety skill knowledge does this juvenile display?
3. What are the factors internal to the juvenile that serve to increase or decrease the likelihood of past or future firesetting?
4. What are the factors external (family, school, community) to the juvenile that serve to increase or decrease likelihood of future firesetting?
5. What is the most responsible risk estimate that can be given for the likelihood of continued firesetting?
6. What services and treatments will serve to reduce risk for future firesetting?

Dr. David Kolko, Director of the Western Psychiatric Institute and Clinic in Pittsburgh, Pennsylvania presented a set of evaluation questions to guide practitioners (Kolko, 1999b):

1. What happened? What is the history of the behavior?
2. Why now? Was (Were) the act(s) intentional or deliberate?
3. Does the child understand the consequences?
4. Does the child have a learning or psychiatric disorder?
5. What outside influences make fire use, exposure, and involvement possible?
6. What is the use of structure, rules, and consequences like in the family?
7. Are parents or family contributing to the problem?

Kolko also identified several domains that are related to the continued efforts towards the development of a risk factor model for assessing firesetting behavior (see Table 8 below; Kolko, 1999b):

TABLE 8: DOMAINS FOR EVALUATION

---

1. Fire incident
2. Fire history
3. Motives and precipitants
4. Consequences/Family discipline
5. Developmental level/IQ
6. Psychiatric disorders and history
7. Family environment
8. Child's cognitive-behavior repertoire
9. Parent functioning and practices
10. Social supports
11. Service availability
12. Treatment outcome

While the cardiac physician and mechanic have at their disposal a set of widely accepted, standardized, and time-tested measures from which they can gather highly reliable data, the same is unfortunately not available for the mental health professional who is faced with the task of completing an assessment of firesetting behaviors. There does not exist a widely accepted, or well articulated set of diagnostic tools, techniques, and strategies specific to firesetting behavior.

In the past two decades investigators have made attempts at using a variety of models as part of their efforts to diagnose firesetting behavior. Investigators have sought to utilize the Wechsler Intelligence Scale for Children, the Bender-Gestalt Test, and the Rorschach (D. Lewis et al., 1980; Ritvo, Shanok, & D. Lewis, 1982) while others have sought to incorporate the use of standardized personality instruments with author-created, fire-specific instruments (Lowenstein, 1981). Last,

Griest, and Kazdin (1985) have explored the development of a multi-dimensional model of assessment that combined the use of both physi-ological and cognitive measures while DeSalvatore and Hornstein (1991) describe the combination of structured fire interviews, a graph-ing technique, and the use of fire-specific projective drawings.

Cole, Grolnick, and Schwartzman (1993) presented a general set of assessment guidelines for professionals in which they recommend that data be gathered from three major sources: a review of the fire incident, completion of a standardized psychiatric interview of the child or adolescent, and completion of a family assessment.

The Arson Prevention Program for Children (TAPP-C), a community-based prevention program based in Ontario, Canada, uti-lizes a fire-risk assessment model that is based upon the hypothesis that "it is the presence of an atypical fire history coupled with a con-comitant child and/or family psychopathology that places a child at specific risk for recidivism firesetting" (p. 299). The TAPP-C assess-ment encompasses investigation in the two major areas of (a) fire-specific behaviors and history and (b) general mental health (Hanson et al., 1995).

Despite the lack of a universal acceptance, there are several firesetting assessment models, protocols, and specific instruments that have been developed and are currently actively utilized by various in-dividuals and professional groups across the country. A review of the assessment models currently in existence reveals a strong and growing consensus among professionals regarding *what* information needs to be gathered and evaluated as part of a firesetting assessment, with greater variation and debate existing as to *how* to gather the informa-tion. A brief review of several of the more popular assessment tools, models, and protocols follows.

Children's Firesetting Interview (CFI) and Firesetting Risk In-terview (FRI). Both the Children's Firesetting Interview (CFI) and the Firesetting Risk Interview (FRI) were developed in an effort to operationalize several domains of functioning, knowledge, and behav-iors that were identified within a "risk factor" model for firesetting previously developed by Kolko and Kazdin (1986). The risk factors that were identified were based on an extensive review of existing mental health and fire service literature and include such factors as (a) early experiences with fire, (b) exposure to models or materials, (c) limited fire safety skills, (d) involvement in antisocial behaviors, (e) motives for the use of fire, (f) exposure to discipline, and (g) poor parental supervision (Kolko & Kazdin, 1989a, 1989b). Internal consistency, test-retest reliability, and criterion validity data were all supportive of the domains which were presented in an *a priori* fashion.

Six domains were identified for the CFI, an instrument that is administered to a child or an adolescent in interview format, and 15 domains were identified for the FRI, a self-report measure completed by parents. On the CFI, firesetters were found to differ from their nonfiresetting counterparts in that they expressed greater curiosity about fire, had greater involvement in fire-related activities, had greater exposure to fire and adult role modeling of fire behaviors, and had greater knowledge of what things will burn. On the FRI, firesetters were found to differ from their nonfiresetting counterparts in that their parents reported greater curiosity about fire, recent involvement in fire-related activities, more frequent expression of negative emotions, greater exposure to others' involvement with fire, and parents' use of harsh discipline practices.

The F.I.R.E. Protocol: An Assessment Instrument for Firesetting Behaviors. Based on experience with over 1,000 cases, authors Irene Pinsonneault and Joseph Richardson developed the F.I.R.E. Protocol as an assessment tool that includes a "Firesetter Interview" and "Risk Evaluation Instrument" (Pinsonneault & Richardson, 1989b). Pinsonneault and Richardson report that the extensive field testing by clinical psychology, probation, fire safety, criminal justice, and educational professionals adds to the reliability of the instrument as a structured guide and its flexibility as an assessment tool. The F.I.R.E. Protocol is described by Pinsonneault and Richardson as a "radical departure from conventional wisdom about both juvenile firesetting as a specific behavior and clinical interviewing a general process" (1989b, p. 1).

The stated goals and objectives of the F.I.R.E. Protocol assessment process are

1. to assess public safety threat to potential victims and community at large.
2. to determine the recidivism risks.
3. to ascertain the nature, extent, and dynamics of the individual's firesetting.
4. to identify specific social, family, environmental, and behavioral treatment needs.
5. to develop specific intervention and treatment recommendations.

The F.I.R.E. Protocol is a step-by-step guide for interviewers, including interview forms, to explore the 10 assessment factors identified by the authors (Pinsonneault & Richardson) as being critical to understanding a child's firesetting behavior (see Table 9 below).

TABLE 9: THE F.I.R.E. PROTOCOL — TEN ASSESSMENT FACTORS

---

1. Child's fire history
2. Child's treatment readiness
3. Child's general personality traits and the relation of these to fire-related behavior
4. Specific fire behaviors
5. Problem fire behaviors
6. Family and school factors
7. Family and fire history
8. Family factors which support/sabotage treatment
9. Honesty and accountability
10. Cooperation with the assessment process

Firesetter Analysis Worksheet. Researchers George Sakheim and Elizabeth Osborn present a Firesetter Analysis Worksheet developed for conducting a firesetting assessment and then arriving at a prediction equation, which they report to be 96% accurate (Sakheim & Osborn, 1994). Based upon the completion of five separate studies completed over a 12-year span, the worksheet defines 25 variables present in a child's or an adolescent's record that have been "consistently and positively" associated with firesetting behavior. In addition, five factors that are seen as indicators for reduced firesetting risk are presented.

Based upon a careful study of a child's or an adolescent's record, a complete history taking, and a recent psychological evaluation and psychiatric examination, Sakheim and Osborn suggest that a clinician is capable of rating the child's or adolescent's status on the individual variables. A "prediction equation," using 14 of the variables included in the worksheet, is then computed to help in determining whether a child or an adolescent is seen as "minor," "moderate," "definite," or "extreme" risk for future firesetting. Sakheim and Osborn (1994) report that 10 variables (e.g., feelings of anger and rejection, feelings of impotent rage, poor judgment in social situations, impulsivity, weak or inadequate superego development, cruelty to animals or children) have emerged as the most predictive of serious risk for firesetting.

Like other practitioners, Sakheim and Osborn point out that their instrument is best used within an integrated analysis of all clinical data and that ultimately there is no substitute for sound, clinical decisions that are based upon the findings or relevant clinical data.

Juvenile Firesetter Needs Assessment Protocol (JFNAP). The more recently developed Juvenile Firesetter Needs Assessment Protocol is described as being appropriate for use with juveniles between the ages of 2 to 18 and is based upon a "mental health-accountability" model that emphasizes victim impact and community safety (Humphreys & Kopet, 1996). The JFNAP was designed for use by mental health professionals as an aid in documenting a juvenile's firesetting history, assessing needs, and making appropriate recommendations for intervention/treatment. Humphreys and Kopet caution against its use as a risk predictive instrument, citing the lack of any reliability and validity data, and they explain that the purpose of this eight-page evaluation format is to (a) assess mental health needs, (b) take an accurate firesetting history, (c) determine precipitating stressors, (d) determine firesetter typology, and (e) make appropriate treatment and supervision recommendations.

The manual for the JFNAP provides an overview of four motivational typologies (curiosity, crisis, delinquent, emotionally disturbed). Humphreys and Kopet propose the following factors as being suggestive of moderate, guarded, or poor prognostic indicators for future firesetting:

Moderate Prognostic Indicators. Nondefensive self-disclosure, acceptance of responsibility, grossly adequate social and psychological adjustment, relatively minor fire history, and parents who are supportive of treatment and capable of increased supervision.

Guarded Prognostic Indicators. Resistance to exploration of fire behaviors and dynamics; prominent careless, reckless, secretive, or impulsive behaviors; low self-esteem, passive-aggressiveness, or criminal thinking patterns; repeated involvement in firesetting behavior; history of trauma or victimization; and parents who are not supportive of firesetter treatment.

Poor Prognostic Indicators. Repeated involvement in firesetting despite treatment, gang or cult involvement, gross delinquent history or presence of major mental illness, motivations of revenge or profit with specific fire targets, cruelty to animals or other assaultive behaviors, history of serious abuse or neglect or other victimization by fire, prominent intellectual deficits or neurological features that have been resistant to medical intervention, and disturbed or chaotic home life.

Humphreys, Kopet, and Lajoy also provide a separate set of 21 recommendations for the caregivers of juvenile firesetters, which encompass the areas of fire prevention measures, family safety rules, fire education, and positive reinforcement (Humphreys et al., 1996).

Qualitative Analysis Model of Child and Adult Fire Deviant Behavior. The impetus for the Qualitative Analysis Model and its three included assessment instruments was the development of the dynamic-behavioral model of firesetting in the early 1980s (Fineman, 1995). Designed as a method to help the forensic evaluator identify the thoughts, behaviors, and feelings that typically are associated with firesetting, the model also proposes a framework for the numerous factors viewed as being related to firesetting.

Fineman reminds practitioners that the successful completion of the three assessment instruments — the Firesetting Sequence Analysis Form, the Firesetting Motive Analysis Form, and the Psycholegal Analysis Form — is based upon an extensive assessment process inclusive of clinical interviews, record review, and psychological testing if necessary.

Fineman proposes a dynamic-behavioral formula for firesetting as:

$$FS = G1 + G2 + E*$$
$$*E = C + CF + D1 + D2 + D3 + F1 + F2 + F3 + Rex + Rin$$

FS = Firesetting behavior

G1 = Dynamic historical factors predisposing the offender to maladaptive behavior

G2 = Historical and current environmental factors that have taught and reinforced firesetting as acceptable

E = Immediate environmental contingencies that encourage firesetting behavior

Includes factors related to immediate precipitant to firestart (C); characteristics of the fire (CF); thinking distortions before, during, and after the fire (D1, D2, D3); feelings before, during, and after the fire (F1, F2, F3); and external and internal reinforcement for the firesetting (Rex and Rin).

The Qualitative Analysis Model emphasizes the thoughts and feelings that accompany fire behavior and incorporates these as the most important factors in the development of a juvenile firesetter intervention strategy. The Firesetting Sequence Analysis Form and the Firesetting Motive Analysis Form are provided as guides for the evaluator during assessment and to provide a format for the evaluator to "clinically weight data as it is acquired in terms of the likelihood of it producing continued firesetting or in terms of its suggesting that the firesetter may harm others or engage in severely destructive property damage" (Fineman, 1995, p. 48). Clinical norms do not currently exist for the weights to be assigned to each item identified as related to firesetting, so it remains the individual evaluator's perception of the risk involved until further study can be accomplished (Fineman, 1995).

MASSACHUSETTS COALITION MODEL

The Massachusetts Statewide Coalition for Juvenile Firesetter Intervention Programs ("the Coalition") is a nonprofit, collaborative organization dedicated to supporting regional and local firesetting intervention programs that have been developed in Massachusetts. All of the programs have been developed within a multidisciplinary model that seeks to establish a framework that provides screening, assessment, and intervention services. The membership of the Coalition is representative of multiple professional disciplines (fire service, law enforcement, juvenile justice, education, social service, and mental health) that are considered to be necessary components of a comprehensive, community-based effort to address juvenile firesetting.

Within the Coalition, I established a Mental Health Task Force (MH Task Force) to be comprised of those psychologists, social workers, and mental health professionals who are involved in a Coalition-sponsored firesetting intervention program or who have dedicated a portion of their professional lives to the juvenile firesetting problem. In 1997, I presented to the members of the MH Task Force the recommendation for a model of the domains I felt needed to be included as part of a comprehensive assessment of firesetting behavior.

This model, based upon an extensive review of the relevant research and clinical experience, was an effort to present the complex nature of the firesetting assessment process through an illustration of the numerous variables that can be related to a particular child's/adolescent's firesetting behavior. It identifies the seven domains believed to be necessary elements for a comprehensive analysis in the completion of a firesetting assessment. Since that time, the model has served as the basis for efforts of the MH Task Force to identify and adopt a standardized assessment model. Each of the domains is considered a distinctly independent variable, lending itself to a variety of data gathering and measurement strategies. Yet each of the domains plays a role in the development of a comprehensive understanding of the entire clinical picture. The domains included are (a) fire history,

(b) fire scene evidence, (c) fire knowledge, (d) parent/family functioning, (e) behavioral functioning, (f) emotional functioning, and (g) cognitive/school functioning.

This visual model (see Figure 1 below) seemed most appropriate and useful as it facilitates the understanding of several fundamental concepts that are critical to the assessment of firesetting behavior. First, firesetting is a complex behavior that is most often the result of the interrelationship of several factors. The assessment process must include gathering information about all of these factors even if they initially appear to be of limited value or if ultimately they are not considered especially critical in the final analysis. An analysis of a juvenile's firesetting behavior based upon information gathered from only one, two, or three domains is rarely sufficient to base an informed opinion about a juvenile's firesetting behavior and creates a risk of missing a potentially key piece of data.

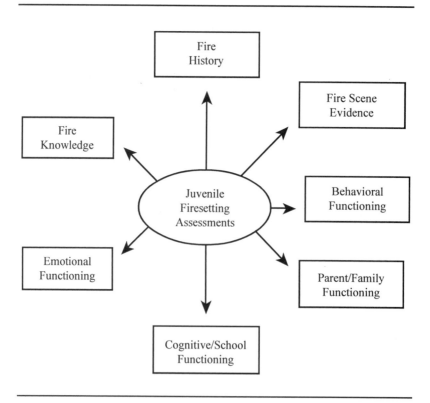

Figure 1. Massachusetts Coalition Model

Second, the population of children and adolescents an evaluator will encounter will be heterogeneous. Unlike purchased jigsaw puzzles that provide a picture of the finished product, a firesetting assessment is like a jigsaw puzzle that comes without a picture to assist in piecing it together. While the assessment may be similar to some of the puzzles you've done before, it will never be exactly the same. As I said before, if you love the challenge of putting complex puzzles together (the diagnostic process), then this is the behavior for you.

Third, the proportion of relevant information coming from each of the domains is as unique as each child or adolescent is unique. For some assessments the largest and most critical pieces of information in analyzing a child's or an adolescent's behaviors come from their extensive and progressive fire history while another child's or adolescent's fire history may be largely unremarkable, having only set one or two fires. For another child the most critical pieces of information related to potential fire risk are revealed in numerous behavioral and emotional indicators while the next child displays a relatively stable behavioral and emotional history. The clinician never knows which domains are most critical until all the data has been reviewed and the location of the most salient information can be determined.

Lastly, to effectively gather data from all of the relevant domains, the clinician must develop a unique combination of knowledge and skills. Evaluators need to be sufficiently capable of performing a variety of interviewing and evaluation functions including (a) detailed history taking; (b) clinical and diagnostic interviewing; (c) administering, scoring, and interpreting behavioral measures; and (d) administering, scoring, and interpreting personality and projective measures. The ability to directly confront attempts at minimization and evasion efforts are especially critical skills when working with older children. In addition, the clinician needs to have a knowledge base in fire chemistry, fire behavior, and fire safety in order to effectively explore, and sometimes challenge, a child's or an adolescent's reported fire behavior.

It is the goal of this author to provide a basic understanding of the firesetting assessment process from which professionals can get direction to more advanced and specific information. The following descriptions of the seven domains of the Massachusetts Coalition Model are presented to (a) provide the clinician with suggested areas of focus in each domain, (b) suggest evaluative questions designed to gather information in fire-specific areas, and (c) describe general psychological measures and tools that might prove helpful.

Fire History. It is a given that a juvenile referred for a firesetting evaluation has set at least one fire in their lifetime, and it is more likely that most have set many more than that. It is typical for evaluators to discover that the number of known or documented fires prior to the assessment is significantly underrepresentative of the actual number of fires in which the child or adolescent has been involved. This is a part of the interview and assessment process that requires a methodical, structured, and detail-oriented manner in order to gather responses that answer the when, where, how, what, and who questions of a juvenile's firesetting history. The goal is quite simple: by the end of the assessment you should know more information about this particular child's or adolescent's fire behaviors than anyone else does.

At the completion of this part of the data collection, an evaluator should have the ability to describe in detail the initiation, sequence, and scope of a child's or an adolescent's fire behavior history. I have found the use of a timeline very helpful in organizing data about fire history. It allows me to actively involve the juvenile in the assessment. Prior to exploring specific fire behavior history, I place several key events on a timeline, beginning with the date of his or her birth and ending with the date of the interview, and explain their relative position on the line. These might include family events (divorce, moves, births), school events (transitions to new schools, entering kindergarten), or other significant life events that the child or adolescent is able to link to a particular time in his or her life. The timeline is then placed between evaluator and juvenile so that each has access to write on the line. I have found that for younger children, or more complex histories, larger pieces of paper provide greater freedom and room for collecting data.

The subjects are then given a red pen or marker and asked to place an (X) on the timeline the first time that they were involved with fire. I will then briefly explore each event in order to see if it is possible to identify precipitants and any details regarding sources of ignition or parental/system responses. The child or adolescent is then asked to place an (X) at the next time he or she was involved, and relevant details for those behaviors are gathered. More details are usually available for fires that have occurred more recently. This same process can be completed with parents or guardians and often the similarity or contrasts of the parent and child or adolescent information provides direction for more detailed interviewing. At times, distinct periods of increased firesetting — or periods of relatively little firesetting activity — emerge that warrant further analysis and interpretation.

Taking a complete history of a juvenile's involvement with fire should provide detailed answers from parents and juveniles to the following questions:

1. When did you become concerned about your child's fire interest or fire behaviors?
2. When did your child first become involved with or interested in fire?
3. What were your responses to the behavior? How effective were your responses?
4. During what periods of your child's life did his or her firesetting occur?
5. Did the behavior progress in its frequency, severity, or complexity?
6. What do you understand as the motive for your child's firesetting?
7. Where did he or she get the matches and lighters that were used?
8. When was your first fire? What happened?
9. When was the second fire? What happened?
10. How many fires have you set?
11. What other ignition sources did you use and at what time?
12. Where have you set fires?
13. Who else was involved with you and your firesetting? When and how did they become involved?

Several of the models and protocols discussed earlier provide graphs or interview guidelines to use (Humphreys & Kopet, 1996; Pinsonneault & Richardson, 1989b) for gathering fire history information. In addition, the Federal Emergency Management Agency (FEMA) has produced the most widely used set of screening measures and tools (for use by fire service personnel predominantly working in community-based programs) that provide interview guidelines for working with juveniles involved in firesetting (FEMA, 1983). Selected portions of the Children's Firesetting Interview (Kolko & Kazdin, 1989b) and Firesetting Risk Interview (Kolko & Kazdin, 1989a) are designed to provide historical and contextual data.

Fire Scene Evidence. The taking of a detailed fire history provides the necessary information to undertake a more detailed analysis of individual fire events that helps in determining specific motives or precipitants for the fire behavior. While the fire history provides answers to the who, what, and when questions, it is the analysis of fire scene evidence that most often provides helpful information regarding "why" the juvenile set a particular fire or a series of fires. Through the gathering of information on the actions, thoughts, and feelings leading up to the fire and the behavioral responses after the fire, the evaluator is provided with a context for developing a hypothesis regarding the motives and understanding of why this particular juvenile was involved with fire.

Information sources for this portion of the assessment can be quite varied, depending on the severity or complexity of the fire. Sometimes information from an arson investigator or juvenile police officer's report can be incorporated. The ability of an arson investigator to provide specialized information from the fire scene that includes the cause and origin of the fire, the rate of fire growth and spread, the presence of accelerants, and the availability of escape routes can prove to be critical pieces of the puzzle. Similarly, the investigating officer's report can provide details about the juvenile's reaction at the fire scene that can prove to be equally as critical. Was the child or adolescent upset by the events? Did he or she make an effort to conceal or minimize his or her involvement? Did he or she leave the scene without attempting to alert other residents or occupants? What did other witnesses report about what happened? It is exactly these types of cases that underscore the need for a multidisciplinary approach and cooperative involvement in addressing the juvenile firesetting problem. If working with fire service, police, or juvenile justice professionals is not appealing to you, then I would urge you to reconsider your position before becoming involved in assessing and treating firesetting behaviors.

The experience of most professionals working with juveniles involved in firesetting is that the large majority of fires which have led to referral for mental health intervention did not involve a formal public safety response on the day of the fire. As a result, fire scene evidence is most often gathered through direct interview with the juveniles themselves and their parents. Given the heterogeneity of the population and the great variety in types and numbers of fires involved, this part of the assessment effort can be either quite simple or quite complex.

It is recommended that the approach and strategies for this portion of the assessment emphasize the ability to reconstruct a child's or an adolescent's actions during a particular fire event in as detailed a manner as possible. Because the desired end result is the evaluator's ability to visualize the child's or adolescent's actions in a sensible way, the evaluator may need to ask the child or adolescent "to walk me through it." While we might find what we hear to be disconcerting, we set as the goal the notion that the reports of their thoughts, feelings, and actions should result in an understandable story. In this portion of the assessment we are attempting as much as possible to hear the juvenile describe his or her actions and the reasons for the actions. Sometimes the sequence of events involves minutes, sometimes hours, and sometimes days.

Depending on the cognitive abilities of the juvenile, the level of cooperation in the interview process, and the amount of planning and premeditation for the fire, the method for gathering fire scene evidence can be quite different. With younger children or those who have limited verbal abilities, you might literally have to have them walk you through it by physically reconstructing the fire scene in your office so they can show you what they did. I remember interviewing a 6-year-old boy who was referred by his mother because in her words "he tried to blow up my car," after he had been found underneath her car with some matches. This very impulsive, learning disabled young man had a difficult time describing the sequence of events leading up to his crawling under his mother's car with some matches and dried up leaves he had found on the street. When we crawled under the coffee table in my office, I handed him a book of matches with the heads removed and several pieces of paper cut out in the shape of leaves. I then told him to show me what he had done, at which point he was able to provide me with the behavioral images I needed to structure my interview questions. He showed me his interest in lighting the leaves on fire with the matches and staying under the car where his mother couldn't see him and he could get away from the cold wind. When asked what was above our heads that might be really dangerous, he had no understanding of the flammability of gasoline and looked quite confused when I tried to explain it to him.

Several authors have provided models or outlines for gathering what we have termed as fire scene evidence. One of the most well known techniques that can provide an evaluator with this data is the Graphing Technique described in 1983 by Bumpass et al. The Graphing Technique involves the use of a vertical axis identifying behavior and external stimuli, and a horizontal axis identifying certain feelings and their intensity. By constructing the graph, the child or adolescent and parents are able to see the correlation between certain stimuli, the feelings that result from the stimuli, and the behaviors that result from the combination of the two. The identification of the sequence of events that led to firesetting in the past provides the opportunity to identify and practice alternative responses. The Firesetting Sequence Analysis and Firesetting Motive Analysis forms by Fineman (1995), and selected questions identified by Barth (1988), Sakheim and Osborn (1994), and Cole et al. (1993) provide additional guidelines for professionals in this portion of the firesetting assessment.

Fire Knowledge. One of the most widely accepted beliefs regarding involvement in irresponsible and dangerous firesetting behavior is that in addition to other variables these juveniles lack appropriate knowledge about fire chemistry, fire behavior, and fire safety procedures. Put in simplest terms, they just do not realize what they are playing with and, as a result, haven't developed the necessary respect for fire and its use. It is the existence of this ignorance of fire and its inherent danger which make it easier for a juvenile to engage in firesetting behavior. The provision of fire safety education is a core component of any intervention program developed to address firesetting behavior at a community level.

Exploring and measuring what juveniles know about fire, do not know about fire, believe they know about fire, or want you to believe they know about fire is the focus of the fire knowledge domain of assessment. This piece of the assessment is heavily content focused and requires a solid level of fire knowledge on the part of the evaluator to explore fully or to challenge strongly held beliefs that a child or an adolescent might have about fire. I would encourage all mental health professionals to explore introductory fire science course opportunities as a first step. One of the worst situations in which to find yourself is to be sitting across the table from a child or an adolescent who has just discovered that he or she knows more about constructing a potato cannon or tennis ball bomb than you do. Having a familiarity with which household products are flammable and which are not, or knowing what happens to plastic toys when they burn, can become a key factor in the successful completion of an assessment. Several years ago I remember being told by a 14 year-old that he would put Vicks Vapo-Rub on his arms and ignite it in front of his friends to impress them and being told by an 11-year-old that he would pour small amounts of butane into his cupped hand and light it with a match to watch it burn. My first reaction, as I sat and listened intently, was to say to myself, "Is that possible?" It wasn't until the interviews ended and I posed the questions to my fire chief that I was given the chemical explanation as to how these behaviors were indeed physically possible.

Published fire knowledge tests (Pinsonneault & Richardson, 1989b) and several fire science curriculums — from which pretests can be constructed — are available. Several of the items on the Children's Firesetting Interview (Kolko & Kazdin, 1989b) are specifically designed to measure fire knowledge. It is also possible to incorporate into the assessment interview several questions and activities to gather a sense of the fire-related knowledge and safety skill awareness the child or adolescent possesses.

These questions may include: Can you define fire? What are the three elements of the fire triangle? What four products do all fires produce? How long do you have to escape a house fire? What are the four classes of fire? I am almost always struck by the gross lack of knowledge demonstrated by these juveniles as it relates to an under-standing of heat and temperature or the skills necessary to escape a structure fire safely. When given a hypothetical fire situation from which to describe their escape, many of these children or adolescents will describe actions that literally would result in their deaths in a mat-ter of seconds. Responses such as "I'd hold my breath and just run through the flames" or "I'd smash the window and throw myself out" are more the rule than the exception. It is these children or adolescents who are almost always at greatest risk for harm in the event of a fire because of the knowledge and skill deficits they possess.

In addition, many of these juveniles come from environments where adults have been poor role models in the fire safety area. Their homes typically lack working smoke detectors, provide unrestricted access to lighters and matches, have no fire escape plan, and are populated with adults whose fire behaviors are at times as problematic as the identi-fied patients. The result is a population of juveniles who, not surpris-ingly, do not have a clue about the potential for harm their behaviors create because they have never been taught.

Parent/Family Functioning. Analyzing the environment in which the firesetting juvenile has been raised can often provide a clearer un-derstanding of the origin, meaning, and context of the specific fire behaviors that a particular juvenile exhibits. It must be emphasized that there exist perfectly normal, high functioning families with chil-dren or adolescents who have been involved in varying levels of fire behavior. An evaluator will encounter parents whose responses to their juvenile's fire behaviors demonstrate (a) adequate concern about the dangers their child's or adolescent's behavior creates, (b) attempts at appropriate behavioral intervention, (c) bewilderment at the behavior's origin, and (d) active seeking of professional assistance. Yet the litera-ture and experience strongly suggest that these types of environments represent a minority in the population of juveniles who have been iden-tified as needing professional intervention. The research literature that has been compiled strongly supports the notion that the parents and families of juveniles engaged in firesetting, when compared to nonfiresetting families, display a set of unhealthy and negative emo-tional and parenting style characteristics (Fineman, 1995; Gale, 1999; Gruber et al., 1981; Kazdin & Kolko, 1986; Kolko & Kazdin, 1990;

Reis, 1993; Sakheim & Osborn, 1994). In fact there is support for the notion that these are some of the most deficited and poorly functioning families one might come across.

Evaluation of the parent and family dynamics is completed through three primary evaluation methods. The first, and typically the most data-rich, is direct clinical interview with both parents. If at all possible, interviewing in the home is strongly suggested in order to allow exposure to the actual physical environment of the family and to have the opportunity to sit with parents in a setting that maximizes their comfort level. The parent interview allows the clinician to gather a sense of the overall emotional climate of the home and to collect data on the existence of family strengths and weaknesses including (a) strength of the marriage relationship, (b) parental discipline styles and practices, and (c) current or previous stressors. Authors have provided suggested formats for family interviewing (Pinsonneault & Richardson, 1989b) within the context of completing a firesetting evaluation. The Firesetting Risk Interview (Kolko & Kazdin, 1989a) includes structured interview responses in the areas of supervision/discipline, parental fire awareness and preparation, and frequency and effectiveness of punishment.

The second source of data from which to gather parent/family functioning data is from the collateral reports of other professionals who have previously or are currently working with the family. This typically includes therapists, social workers, teachers, and police and fire investigators who are able to provide firsthand information about working with a particular family. My experience is that an evaluator needs to be appropriately cautious in remaining objective during the assessment process and base any final findings on the compilation of relevant and sufficient data from which analysis can be made. Although parents and families will tend to display a certain style of relating to professionals over time, as individuals do, there are times when the combination of the professional and family can result in a unique set of relationship difficulties or strengths. Relationships are often complex, and with complex families they can be even more difficult to predict and maintain.

I recently had the opportunity to interview a social worker from a secure treatment facility who was able to describe to me in great detail her approach and style with the mother of a 12-year-old boy for whom I had been asked to complete a firesetting evaluation. The year previous the family had removed this young boy from a prior placement because of a rather rapid deterioration of the family's relationship with the treatment program and loss of trust in the program staff. Since his admission to his current program, the relationship with the mother had been rebuilt based upon the social worker's insight and her ability to respect the mother's role as a primary decision maker. Over the course of his placement, the strength of this parent-professional bond had allowed the treatment team the ability to confront and overcome some very difficult issues that needed to be addressed. Although I did not have the chance to interview staff from the prior placement, a placement that lasted for only 2 weeks, I am sure I would have heard quite a different interpretation of this particular family's strengths and weaknesses. During the course of evaluation and treatment, an evaluator will frequently encounter families who repeat a longstanding pattern of either positive or negative interactions. There are, however, times when an evaluator's experience with a family greatly differs from that of another professional. It is this difference that becomes grist for the assessment mill.

The final source of parent/family functioning information comes from the incorporation of the use of standardized measures in the assessment process. Published tools, such as the Parental Stress Index (Abidin, 1995), provide the ability to include objective data regarding the self-reported impact of various stressors on the parental functioning of juveniles involved in firesetting. By combining observations, collateral reports, and historical information, mental health professionals have at their disposal sufficient material from which to develop accurate and sound interpretations and, more importantly, treatment recommendations that maximize potential success.

Behavioral Functioning. At its root, juvenile firesetting is a behavioral problem. In fact, two of the three most frequently reported diagnostic categories among the entire population of juveniles that engage in firesetting behavior, ADHD and Conduct Disorder, are disorders characterized by behavior. The ability of the evaluator to assess a child's or an adolescent's behavioral functioning is a core component of the firesetting assessment. How juveniles have behaved in the past and how they have responded to previous interventions is largely predictive of their future behavior pattern. A child or an adolescent whose firesetting is one of a number of chronic problematic and dangerous behaviors is a very different presentation, and presents different challenges, than the one who, aside from his or her firesetting, is described as compliant and displays a history that is negative for behavioral problems. Due to the varied nature of this population of juveniles, reported histories of behavior problems are likely to run the gamut from nonexistent to extensive and complex. Taking as complete a history as possible, including the chronicling of behavior problems involving sibling and family relationships, peers and friendships, school and work functioning, and any police/court involvement, provides the necessary behavioral context for understanding a juvenile's firesetting behavior. In addition to behavioral history, how the juvenile is currently or recently behaving or the existence of distinct periods of deterioration or improvement in behavior needs to be taken into account.

Evaluators should concentrate on answering the following questions related to a juvenile's behavioral history:

1. Are the behavior problems acute or chronic? What has been the rate of progression?
2. Does there exist consensus between more than one source as to scope and severity?
3. Does the child's or adolescent's behavior reflect significant impulsivity?
4. Has the juvenile been charged with any criminal behavior?
5. Is the child's or adolescent's behavior different according to setting, time, or environmental factors?
6. Are there possible developmental factors impacting behavior functioning?
7. Has the child or adolescent displayed any offending or aggressive behaviors towards people? Animals?
8. Have there been distinct periods of increased or decreased behavior problems?

Several empirically validated behavior measures are available to mental health professionals from which to gather both parent and teacher reports of behavioral symptoms and their severity. A review of the program and research data and my own experience indicate that professionals working with juveniles involved in firesetting have adapted the use of several established behavioral measures as part of their firesetting intervention work. These include the parent and teacher versions of the Child Behavior Checklist (Achenbach & Edelbrock, 1983), the Conner's Rating Scale-Revised (Conners, 1997), and the Behavior Assessment System for Children or BASC (Reynolds & Kamphaus, 1996). All three measures, although somewhat distinct in development, provide clinicians with detailed descriptions of levels of behavioral symptoms across a number of clinically validated subscales. Also available for professionals working with specialized populations are behavior measures that address more localized constellations of behavioral symptoms. Examples include the Overt Aggression Scale (Yudofsky, 1986) for delinquent/violent populations and the Trauma Symptom Checklist for Children — TSCC (Briere, 1996) for children and adolescents with known or suspected histories of trauma and abuse. The use of such measures, in combination with behavior history and clinical observation of current behavioral functioning, provides a solid foundation from which to develop intervention strategies.

Emotional Functioning. Some juveniles are involved with fire for reasons that are quite personal. In the end, their firesetting behaviors are interpreted as being related to, or comorbid with, their experience of very painful, lonely, anxious, depressed, angry, or fearful feelings. Others suffer from the emotional damage their firesetting behaviors have created. As the population of juveniles involved in firesetting is quite heterogeneous, the emotional and psychiatric problems presented by these juveniles, and the relationship of these problems to their firesetting behavior, will be quite diverse. The diagnostic question an evaluator is attempting to clarify is whether there are characteristics of this child's or adolescent's emotional functioning that might serve, or have already served, to increase or decrease their likelihood of being involved in firesetting behavior.

Some of the juveniles involved in firesetting are the saddest and most anxious individuals you will meet. An 11-year-old boy with no prior history of firesetting or problem behaviors cries uncontrollably as he explains that he didn't mean to burn and permanently disfigure his 5-year-old brother's arm. Through his tears he explains that he was just trying to show him a "trick" with hairspray and a match that he heard about in school that day and that his brother got too close and tried to grab the can of hairspray. When his brother's sleeve caught fire, he reports running as fast as he could to get his mother, but by the time they returned to the room, his brother's arm was so severely burned that he couldn't even look. Yet there are those whom the evaluator meets that are some of the most aggressive, violent, and dangerous young offenders in our youth correctional facilities or secure treatment centers. The 13-year-old who sits across the table coldly and justifiably explaining his reasons for pouring gasoline on a young girl's hair and setting it on fire. Or the 16-year-old, disturbed by the tone of your voice and the content of your interview, who leans across the table and cooly explains that he saw the car you drove up in, will find out where you live, and will burn your house to the ground if he gets the chance.

The task of clinically assessing the emotional functioning of children or adolescents, like the assessment of their behavioral and cognitive functioning, is facilitated by the existence of a number of well-established and empirically validated strategies, tools, and measures. The use of these more generic measures and techniques with the firesetting population is accomplished quite readily. The incorporation of the use of personality and projective measures in a firesetting assessment is based upon the assumption that the clinician has received adequate training and demonstrated a level of proficiency and skill with the measures through supervised experience.

At the core of the assessment of emotional functioning is the direct clinical interview and observation of the child or adolescent by the clinician. How children or adolescents relate in interview, describe their relationships and actions, or describe the impact of events on themselves provides an evaluator with some of the richest data available. Skilled diagnostic interviewing remains the most valuable tool in the mental health professional's assessment toolbox. Likewise, the clinical impressions and findings of prior or current providers can prove to be a critical source of data, and every effort should be made to review prior psychological and psychiatric evaluations and to consult with appropriate professionals.

In addition to diagnostic data gathered through direct clinical interview, collateral consult, and previous evaluations, there are numerous personality and projective measures that have been used by researchers and practitioners in work with the juvenile firesetting population, including the MMPI-A, Sentence Completion Test, Rorschach Inkblot Test, and the Children's Hostility Inventory (DeSalvatore & Hornstein, 1991; Kolko & Kazdin, 1991a; Moore et al., 1996). Given the significant representation of the diagnosis of Conduct Disorder in the firesetting population, the use of personality measures normed on a delinquent population shows particular promise for use in firesetting assessment work. The Jesness Inventory, a 155-item self-report personality measure, has been designed for use in the classification and treatment of disturbed children and adolescents (Jesness, 1996). The Jesness Inventory provides scores on 11 personality characteristics (e.g., social maladjustment, immaturity, manifest aggression, denial) and also provides the ability to classify into one or more of 9 delinquent personality subtypes. The Jesness Inventory has been endorsed for use with adolescent sex offender populations (Perry & Orchard, 1992) and has been used in treatment effectiveness studies of inpatient delinquent populations (Roberts et al., 1990).

Cognitive/School Functioning. The final domain identified for assessment in the Massachusetts Coalition Model is that of intellectual and academic functioning. While often overlooked, or minimized in its importance, the cognitive abilities of a child or an adolescent are a critical variable of study when one is attempting to construct an understanding of past behaviors and actions and/or a treatment plan for the future. A child or an adolescent whose latest standardized intelligence score measures 80 or less on the verbal scale is not only in need of an adapted interview style but is also in need of selected treatment strategies designed to be appropriate to their verbal ability level. It has been my experience, and the experience of many of my colleagues, that we are most likely to encounter children and adolescents who are less verbally developed than nonverbally developed on standard IQ measures and who often have documented histories of learning disabilities in the language area. Not surprisingly, in interview it is typically much easier for these children and adolescents to show you what they did, via role-play or drawings, than to tell you what they did with their words. They are behavioral communicators, which is why firesetting is sometimes so appealing to them. It is a great communicator.

The assessment of a child's or an adolescent's cognitive and school functioning is accomplished through relatively straightforward methods. First, as an evaluator you will have your own mental status impressions of the child or adolescent based upon clinical interview. Does he or she seem to understand the questions being asked? Does he or she display poor ability to recall data or events? Does he or she struggle with questions that ask him or her to think abstractly about feelings or motivations? Is his or her language ability delayed or impoverished? Does he or she seem confused? Secondly, an evaluator is strongly encouraged to review prior evaluations for results on standardized IQ measures (Wechsler Intelligence Scale for Children-Third Edition, Wechsler Adult Intelligence Scale-Third Edition) and performance on academic achievement testing. Third, an evaluator can gather reports from teachers and school personnel regarding past and current school performance and the existence of any behavioral problems that may or may not be related to school difficulties.

TREATMENT OF JUVENILE
FIRESETTING BEHAVIOR

REVIEW OF LITERATURE

The sparse body of available literature related to the treatment of firesetting behavior falls into three categories: (a) case study descriptions of various treatment programs designed for individual children or adolescents with firesetting behavior, (b) programmatic descriptions of community-based, multidisciplinary initiatives developed to provide screening, assessment, and intervention services, and (c) descriptions of inpatient and outpatient treatment protocols within mental health facilities. According to McGrath, Marshall, and Prior (1979), the majority of behavioral researchers up until the late 1970s had used electrical aversion therapy as the principal or only component in the treatment of firesetting behavior in juveniles. The relatively limited firesetting treatment literature that currently exists, not surprisingly, includes the use of intervention and treatment strategies that are as unique and heterogeneous as the population of juveniles involved in the behavior. This diverse collection of treatment literature includes the description of the application of multiple family therapy strategies, social skills training, several behavior modification techniques, psychoanalytic therapy, hypnosis, satiation techniques, fire station visits, fire safety education, pharmacotherapy, hospitalization, and others.

While the majority of the early treatment literature (pre-1990) presented information in single subject, case study format, there appears to have been early recognition of the need for highly individualized, comprehensive, and sometimes alternative treatment strategies for firesetting behavior. McGrath et al. (1979) developed a three phase (intensive, transitional, follow-up) "comprehensive" treatment program for an 11-year-old boy. Kolko (1983) described the use of "multicomponent parental treatment" of firesetting with a boy displaying significant developmental disabilities. In working with a 10-year-old boy with a history of severe behaviors, Koles and Jenson (1985) described the development of an extensive treatment program, based upon motivational and contextual assumptions, that included social skills training, relaxation training, overt sensitization, fire safety education, overcorrection procedures, and behavioral contracting.

Carstens (1982), in somewhat of a departure from this comprehensive approach, advocated the more simple application of a work penalty behavioral technique where the child or adolescent was required to complete 1 hour of hard labor for every incident of firesetting behavior. Several practitioners advocated the use of "controlled firesetting" with the assistance of a therapist as a form of therapeutic intervention (Jones, 1981). A report on the use of this "alternative therapy" with a 10-year-old boy who had not responded to 2 years of individual therapy, family therapy, and fire safety education within a psychiatric hospital reported that:

It was as though the therapist's presence during the fire interrupted M's usual ritual and made it difficult for him to relieve his tension via fire setting. M learned that with appropriate forethought and planning the fire could be controlled in reality. He did not have to turn to fantasy to achieve a sense of mastery over the fire. (Dalton, Haslett, & Daul, 1986, p. 716)

A treatment regimen inclusive of fire safety/prevention skills training, parent training in behavior management, individual therapy, and pharmacotherapy was described as successful (i.e., no fire behaviors at 1-year follow-up) for a young boy from a highly dysfunctional family (Cox-Jones et al., 1990). Zingaro and Pittman-Wagers (1992) presented a case study description on their use of hypnosis, in conjunction with family therapy, in the treatment of a 6-year-old boy with a 1-year history of firesetting behavior. Zingaro and Pittman-Wagers describe the successful use of hypnosis as a strategy to aid in the patient's development of more adaptive cognitive schemes, which then could be reinforced in the work with the family. Clare et al. (1992) reported that at 4-month follow-up there was no firesetting behavior exhibited by a young man who had undergone facial surgery and who participated in a treatment regimen including functional analysis, social skills training, assertion training, relaxation, and covert sensitization. A hospital-based program reported that at 1-year follow-up only 1 out of 35 children, or 2.8%, who had participated in a "Smokey the Bear" firesetting intervention program was found to have set another fire (DeSalvatore & Hornstein, 1991).

While the various multimodal treatment approaches described above were being developed within the more traditional mental health framework and settings (hospitals and clinics), there were a number of professionals strongly advocating for increased mental health involvement in community-based intervention programs. They encouraged the need for increased multidisciplinary cooperation in collaborative efforts with fire service and juvenile justice personnel (Fineman, 1980; Gaynor & Hatcher, 1987; Wooden & Berkey, 1984). The majority of early community-based efforts were developed within guidelines that were created by one of two national programs. The United States Federal Emergency Management Agency (FEMA) pioneered the development and use of screening, assessment, and classification tools to be used primarily by trained local firefighters working in local intervention programs (FEMA, 1979, 1983). In addition to these FEMA training and program materials, the "Firehawks" Program — originally developed by the National Firehawk Foundation in cooperation with the San Francisco, California, Fire Department — incorporated a unique component (Gaynor, McLaughlin, & Hatcher, 1984). The "Firehawk's" Program included an effort to match trained firefighters with identified younger firesetters in a mentoring relationship.

Subsequent efforts at developing intervention programs for juvenile firesetting relied heavily upon the training methods, materials, and philosophies of these two early programs (Baizerman & Emshoff, 1984; Bumpass, Brix, & Preston, 1985; Webb et al., 1990). In a 1988 survey study of 16 FEMA programs and 13 Firehawk-based programs, Kolko noted the importance of several program components of these fire department-based intervention programs. These include (a) interventions based upon strong conceptual models and procedures that were empirically supported, (b) assessment of child and family variables associated with firesetting, (c) provision of fire safety education, and (d) formal program evaluation and outcome data (Kolko, 1988). These early efforts to develop multidisciplinary and community-based programs laid the foundation for several statewide models for screening, assessment, and program development strategies that are increasingly serving as local service delivery models (Massachusetts Coalition for Juvenile Firesetter Intervention Programs, 1999; Oregon State Fire Marshal, 1996). Kolko (1999b) identified six implementation components for a successful community-based firesetting intervention program including (a) educating parents on effective prevention, (b) identifying the child's family role and motives, (c) attending to parent/family resources and stressors, (d) screening for additional problems and making appropriate referrals, (e) providing comprehensive fire education and safety skills training, and (f) evaluating outcomes and program operations. Similarly, the Massachusetts Coalition recommends the adoption of service elements and program components identified by the acronym "SMART" (Massachusetts Coalition for Juvenile Firesetter Intervention Programs, 1999):

S	=	Specialized services delivered by trained professionals
M	=	Multidisciplinary involvement of fire service, juvenile justice, law enforcement, mental health, and social service professionals
A	=	Accountability through evaluation and clear guidelines
R	=	Range of services that can provide a continuum of care
T	=	Triage process for all decision making

There are very few available empirical studies that have used comparison or control study methods to explore the effectiveness of mental health interventions or fire safety education programs. Kolko,

Watson, and Faust (1991) randomly assigned hospitalized children to two treatment groups — group fire safety/prevention skills training (FSST) and individual fire awareness discussion (FAD). FSST involvement was reported to result in lowered contact with fire-related toys, increased fire knowledge, and reduced fire involvement at a 6-month follow-up. Researchers from Australia randomly assigned firesetters (ages 5-16) to various treatment conditions based on their classification as either curious or pathological (Adler et al., 1994). Curiosity firesetters were assigned to either home-based fire education services or a combined treatment/education condition. Pathological cases were offered mental health services in addition to one of the two treatment conditions. While both groups demonstrated significant reductions in firesetting activity, there were no significant differences between home-based fire education and the combined treatment methods. Adler et al. stressed that even minimal intervention may have a beneficial effect in reducing firesetting behavior over a long period of time.

A similar study conducted by Kolko (1996) compared the efficacy of a brief home visit by a firefighter (FHV) to a more formal fire safety education (FSE) and to psychosocial treatment services (PT) provided in a clinic. All of the interventions were designed to (a) be short term, (b) involve both the children and parents, and (c) be delivered by trained professionals. All three treatment conditions resulted in dramatic declines in firesetting behaviors with some support of additional effect provided by the FSE and PT conditions.

Despite the limitations of the treatment literature available, the experience of mental health professionals working with firesetting behavior indicates that treatment interventions that specifically address firesetting behavior appear to result in lowered rates of recidivism, estimated at approximately 10% (Kolko, 1985; Kolko et al., 1991; Stadolnik, 1999). Porth (1997) highlighted fire department statistics of 6.2% recidivism based on a mailing and phone follow-up strategy.

Becoming involved in the treatment of firesetting behavior requires of the mental health professional an acceptance of certain pragmatic, professional practice, and personal realities. Pragmatically, the goal of any professional involvement in firesetting treatment must always remain simple and direct — to eliminate all irresponsible and dangerous firesetting behaviors. Any efforts by children, adolescents, parents, or other professionals to minimize the seriousness of the behavior must be dealt with directly. The clear communication of this goal to firesetting children, adolescents, and their families needs to be incorporated into a professional's interviewing and intake practices. A counselor's ability to confidently explain to a family and child or adolescent that a singular focus on the elimination of all firesetting behavior is not only warranted but nonnegotiable given the inherent danger and potential destructiveness of their decision making, establishes a necessary treatment structure for many of the chaotic and disorganized families that are encountered. For those children and adolescents whose firesetting appears less severe or problematic, the directed manner in which this is presented as the treatment goal is usually quite comforting to a frightened and concerned parent.

While the professional's establishment of a "zero tolerance" philosophy for firesetting behavior remains singular and focused, the actual treatment methods and strategies utilized to reach that goal are as diverse and unique as the children or adolescents involved in the behavior. The identification and implementation of the appropriate treatment strategy for a child or an adolescent is dependent upon factors that include firesetting motives and history, family dynamics, diagnostic profile, and the availability of treatment resources. There is growing evidence that supports a treatment plan of basic fire safety education and parent consultation for juveniles whose fire behaviors are deemed as being relatively low risk (Sakheim & Osborn, 1994). Yet there has simultaneously developed a growing recognition of the need for specialized residential placements and other intensive intervention programs for juveniles whose firesetting behaviors present as imminently dangerous to themselves or others.

TREATMENT COMPONENTS

There currently does not exist a set of widely recognized, standardized, and empirically validated treatment protocols for firesetting behavior available to mental health professionals. Given the diverse treatment needs of this population, it is more realistic for researchers and practitioners to think in terms of the development and application of multiple treatment options, or pathways, and the need for collaboration among the different delivery systems. The efficiency of the delivery and coordination of an array of services has been identified as one of the most critical elements in future development of treatment networks that address firesetting behavior (Kolko, 1999a). The ability to provide treatment and intervention services for firesetting behavior requires a set of diverse assessment, treatment, and interpersonal skills. While efforts continue to further clarify the often complex set of variables related to a juvenile's ultimate involvement in firesetting behavior, numerous literature-supported strategies and applications currently represent what could be considered "best practice" methods of treatment and intervention. The formulation of a treatment plan designed to meet an individual juvenile's needs should incorporate strategies that (a) specifically address elimination of the firesetting behavior, (b) target family and environmental characteristics that support firesetting, (c) improve skill deficits in social, emotional, or academic functioning, and (d) improve the level of fire safety knowledge and appropriate fire safety skills.

The Oregon Treatment Strategies Task Force (1996), through the development of a Cycles Model of Firesetting, recommends that four areas of a child's or an adolescent's functioning/environmental context be addressed when determining a treatment plan. These include (a) emotional and cognitive functioning, (b) behavioral functioning, (c) family and household environment, and (d) community/social environment. The mental health practitioner involved in firesetting treatment and intervention will need to develop the ability to participate in some or all of the various intervention strategies discussed below.

Fire Service Collaboration. This complex population of juveniles is increasingly believed to be best served through an array of services provided by community-based, collaborative intervention programs that capitalize on the expertise of fire service, law enforcement, education, and mental health professionals (Bumpass et al., 1985; Cole et al., 1993; Kolko, 1999a; Sakheim & Osborn, 1994). Most often referred to as JFIP's (Juvenile Firesetting Intervention Programs), these collaborative and multidisciplinary efforts have been established across the country at the local, county, and state levels (see Appendix, pp. 81-84) and are typically created from leadership and coordination provided by fire service professionals. As a mental health provider, being a member of an intervention team has advantages that far outweigh any benefits from working in relative isolation with firesetting behavior. Those who relish their professional independence, autonomy, and ability to make unfettered treatment decisions are likely to find firesetting behavior an area of work that results in unavoidable conflicts with the other disciplines involved. As Kolko (1999a) states,

> Multidisciplinary collaboration in the administration of services for firesetting youth has become an important advance in this area and, in recent years, represents more the rule than the exception. This is due, in part, to accumulation of evidence suggesting the relevance of fire safety and mental health considerations in understanding the problem of juvenile firesetting,

and to the recognition of the roles being played by professionals in the juvenile justice, burn care, and other medical, educational, and social service systems. (p. 109)

Multidisciplinary efforts are often difficult to establish and maintain. The fields of mental health and fire service have had little opportunity and experience with collaborative efforts. While this might be
attributable to the fact that the central mission of each of these disciplines is vastly different from the other, it has been my experience that
there exists a level of professional ignorance, and even elitism, within
both groups. Very few mental health professionals have an understanding of the professional motivations, personal values, and professional
ideals that most firefighters possess. Nor do most mental health professionals appreciate and respect the often tremendous emotional pres-
sure firefighters experience and the impact their work life has on their
emotional and cognitive style as well as their interpersonal functioning. This is a profession, although firefighters more often describe it as
a "brotherhood," which involves the repetitive exposure to traumatic
events (e.g., extractions from car accidents, fire fatalities, severe burn
injuries) year after year. I have been told many times by firefighters
and officers — and I believe it is true — that unless one is a firefighter,
a person just cannot understand. Conversely, very few firefighters understand or appreciate the work of most psychologists and social workers and the professional motivations, skills, and values that we hold as
a professional group. From a professional practice vantage point, it is
of critical importance that mental health professionals involved in
firesetting firmly adopt an orientation where they see themselves, and
the professional services they offer, as part of a network of interdepen-
dent intervention services for children and families.

Coordination of mental health intervention services with services
available from the fire service offers a number of benefits when working with the juvenile firesetting population. Fire departments, predominantly through an identified fire prevention officer, have long been the
source for fire safety education programs for juveniles. Research has
suggested that firefighters are generally perceived by the public as the
professional group that would likely be contacted for child or adolescent fire safety information and firesetter resource information (Winget
& Whitman, 1973). Primary prevention education programs, typically
offered to kindergarten and early elementary school age children (1st
and 2nd grades), focus upon specific fire safety skills (e.g., crawl low
in smoke; stop, drop, and roll). Increasing numbers of fire department
personnel are receiving advanced training and are developing fire safety

curriculums as part of secondary prevention programs for juveniles who have been identified as having been involved in firesetting behavior. When a professional is faced with the task of attempting to access fire safety education services for a child or an adolescent and family, the local fire department is usually the first, and most often the best, resource to be contacted.

Fire departments are often quite willing to work closely with a parent and family to improve the fire safety environment of a home. Fire prevention officers will frequently offer to complete a safety inspection of the home, replace or provide smoke detectors and fire extinguishers, or provide written or video educational materials to parents on fire safety. Several of the strategies recommended to families as means of improving the fire safety environment of the home can be accomplished most readily by fire service professionals (Humphreys et al., 1996). Another benefit of coordination of services with local fire departments is the mental health professional's access to the wide base of knowledge that firefighters typically possess about fire chemistry, fire behavior, fire suppression, and incendiaries/explosives.

Coordination with the fire department and other law enforcement agencies also provides the opportunity to develop within an intervention program a higher level of restrictiveness and coercion for families and juveniles whose resistance, or refusal, to participate in identified services is viewed as a potential public safety threat. The formal and legal authority of a fire chief, police detective, or arson investigator can produce treatment compliance in some of the most difficult and resistant families. While the need for this type of intervention typically occurs within the seriously delinquent and recalcitrant subpopulation of the overall juvenile firesetting population, it is sometimes the only difference between treatment success and failure. Community-based programs require a coordinated set of policies, procedures, and task descriptions for police, fire service, and juvenile justice personnel in order to meet the complex needs of this population.

Because of their centralized position and ability to respond immediately, fire service professionals, after receiving training, often provide a "screening" function in community-based programs providing assessment and treatment services. This is typically accomplished through the use of structured interview tools, administered by paraprofessionals, and designed to help in the identification of juveniles who are in need of varying levels of intervention services (FEMA, 1983). There are, however, concerns that have been raised, and are as yet unanswered, as to the accuracy of this methodology. Pierce and Hardesty

(1997) found that over half of the children and adolescents screened for intervention services by fire service professionals, who received clinically significant psychopathology scores on a standardized behavior checklist, were not referred for mental health services as part of their intervention plan. These findings would support the need for increased collaboration between the disciplines and the need for more critically objective rating instruments to be made available to fire service professionals.

Fire Safety Education. Providing firesetting juveniles access to a comprehensive and professionally delivered fire safety education/skills program as part of a treatment intervention strategy has been consistently supported in mental health literature (Barth, 1988; Cole et al., 1993; Grolnick et al., 1990; Kolko et al., 1991; Raines & Foy, 1994). There has also been support for the notion that, regardless of the extent or seriousness of the fire behavior displayed by a juvenile, their participation in a fire safety education program that promotes safe fire use should be considered a mandatory component of treatment (Cole et al., 1993; Stadolnik, 1998b). The effectiveness of fire safety education is enhanced when programs (a) are delivered in individual or group format by trained instructors; (b) are based upon established curriculums and teaching practices; (c) avoid the use of fear-inducing techniques; (d) are developmentally appropriate to the juvenile's level of functioning; (e) incorporate parent education strategies designed to reduce access to ignition sources, increase supervision, and increase parents' sense of control and safety; and (f) utilize evaluation measures as part of curriculum. Numerous published curriculums, like the Learn Not to Burn Program (NFPA, 1992), are available from several of the resources listed in the appendix section of this book (pp. 81-84).

Children and adolescents who are curious about fire are best served by being provided with accurate information about the dangers of fire and opportunities to practice such safety skills as "crawl low in smoke" and "stop, drop, and roll." Based on this premise, formal fire safety education programs have been created to meet this need. In addition, fire safety education programs address the needs of juveniles whose firesetting behavior is driven by motivations other than, or in addition to, curiosity. Children and adolescents whose firesetting behavior is interpreted as being related to efforts to control or master their environment through fire are offered an opportunity to master fire through increased knowledge and skill development. It is not uncommon for us to tell children/adolescents that prior to leaving our fire safety education program they will know more about fire than anyone else in their school or grade. In addition, juveniles who are involved in antisocial firesetting behavior that causes damage or destruction of property and results in a juvenile justice intervention can be held responsible for successful completion of a fire safety education as part of their diversion or court-sanctioned requirements. In these instances, satisfactory performance on a course evaluation measure or posttest, and compliance with strict behavioral and attendance guidelines, are established requirements of the program with severe sanctions identified for non-compliance.

Behavioral Interventions. Application of behavior therapy techniques for juvenile firesetting is the oldest and most common method of treatment intervention (Raines & Foy, 1994). Individual treatment methods have included the use of a variety of response-cost, punishment, contingency reinforcement, and satiation strategies designed to eliminate fire behaviors and to encourage more appropriate fire behaviors. The level of behavioral intervention that is necessary is dependent on the chronicity and seriousness of the behavioral problems the juvenile exhibits.

Several of the strategies that have been described in the literature are designed to help children identify the ways in which they have used their firesetting as a response to certain situations through the identification of antecedents (Bumpass et al., 1983; Cole et al., 1993; Kolko & Ammerman, 1988). If the therapist is able to create a climate that allows the child or adolescent to openly explore the sequence of events and the cognitions and feelings that occurred simultaneous to each event, it allows for the opportunity to develop a set of alternative responses. A "graphing technique," described by Bumpass et al. (1983), has been used with firesetting children or adolescents and their parents. It involves the construction of a visual image of the firesetting sequence. By plotting events on the vertical axis and feelings and thoughts on the horizontal axis, the child or adolescent and family are shown the likely sequence and trigger events, which then can become a focus for intervention. Role-play, behavioral rehearsal, didactic discussion, and the use of videotaped vignettes have also been used to inhibit anti-social responses and replace them with more prosocial responses.

Group programs that incorporate more traditional cognitive-behavioral intervention techniques are being specifically developed for use with children and adolescents involved in firesetting behavior. This methodology appears to hold promise with the Conduct Disordered and Oppositional Defiant Disordered population of children and adolescents, inclusive of numbers of firesetting children and adolescents who (a) tend to display difficulties in anticipating consequences of their behaviors, (b) tend to perceive aggressive cues in normal situations, (c) underperceive their own level of aggression, and (d) expect aggression to work, valuing the qualities of dominance and revenge (Hollin, 1990; Kazdin, 1997; Lochman, 1992). Campbell and Elliot (1996) have created a skill-based program specifically for 13- to 18-year-old firesetters that incorporates the use of a graph technique with lessons designed to address (a) assertiveness, (b) communication, (c) anger control, (d) conscience and thinking errors, and (e) development of a relapse prevention plan.

Other cognitive-behavioral and psychoeducational intervention strategies have sought to address the social skill deficits and peer relationship difficulties that characterize many of the juveniles involved in firesetting. Treatment programs that incorporate efforts to increase the effectiveness of peer relationships by the use of assertiveness training and by identifying the thoughts and feelings that have precipitated angry outbursts at peers have been used for firesetters (Koles & Jenson, 1985).

The application of behavioral techniques utilizing satiation or over-practice strategies as part of a more comprehensive intervention received early attention by researchers (Koles & Jenson, 1985; Kolko & Ammerman, 1988; McGrath et al., 1979) but appear to have received little application in the past decade. The practice of having a child or an adolescent repeatedly ignite and extinguish hundreds of matches at a time, or the setting of controlled fires in the presence of parents or a therapist, has raised significant concerns of their practicality and application (Cole et al., 1993). A review of the current literature fails to identify the existence of a multidisciplinary program or hospital-based program that continues to utilize satiation strategies as part of its intervention services. Conversely, positive practice and programs that reinforce appropriate fire behavior (e.g., "find a match, find a grown up"), as well as punishment strategies for irresponsible fire use (i.e., response-cost or work penalty), seemingly remain popular.

Family Therapy. As noted earlier, the families of firesetting children and adolescents, when compared to their nonfiresetting counterparts, display a set of negative characteristics that include (a) higher levels of stress coupled with minimal problem-solving skills, (b) increased affective distress and marital discord among parents, (c) greater use of harsh and rigid discipline techniques, and (d) decreased levels of supervision, structure, and rule enforcement (Fineman, 1995; Gale, 1999; Kolko & Kazdin, 1990; Reis, 1993; Sakheim & Osborn, 1994).

Interventions with the parents and families of juvenile firesetters tend to target several areas of concern. These families are often characterized as being highly disorganized, chaotic, and able to provide only minimal supervision. They are multiproblem, complex, and high-risk families. The application of structural family therapy techniques, the provision of intensive levels of home-based support, and the marshaling of community resources (after-school programs, day care, respite) are often necessary to establish stability in the home. Frequently a therapist will encounter a single parent female, with limited financial or emotional resources, feeling overwhelmed by the task of raising children or adolescents who are exhibiting significant behavioral and emotional problems of their own. These are homes where there is little sense of containment, safety, predictability, or structure. In these instances, particularly with a cooperative adult(s), a parent support and guidance approach may provide an avenue to bolster the ability of parents to create a more structured and stable family environment.

Families of problematic firesetters are often characterized by environments where discipline methods are developmentally inappropriate, adults lack appropriate judgment and perspective, and parents have difficulty in modulating their responses to their child's or adolescent's behavior. Parents may practice the harshest, most rigid, sometimes abusive, punishment techniques. I have met parents who staunchly defended their having burned their child's finger with a match or having extinguished a lit cigarette on an arm as their best effort to "show him how dangerous it is!" In contrast, parents of problematic firesetters also include the most lax of disciplinarians whose nonresponsiveness to their children's or adolescent's behavior borders on neglect. These parents' inaction allows the continuation of verbal or physical attacks of themselves, siblings, and neighbors to escalate to dangerous levels. Practitioners must be comfortable and familiar with the abuse and neglect reporting statutes of their own state and have an understanding of the use of such reporting as an intervention strategy. Many of the parents in these families have themselves been raised in chaotic, violent, and inappropriate conditions that leave them ill equipped to parent effectively. Parent training programs, structural family therapy techniques, and generic problem-solving techniques may be beneficial in ameliorating these negative conditions and improving parent discipline skills. Often these families have been involved in multiple treatment and intervention services prior to a firesetting incident, with varying levels of success, and at times are difficult to engage. Mahoney (1999) noted the difficulties that firesetting families have in maintaining gains made in therapy and the significant concerns regarding high therapy dropout rates. The need for coercive alternatives to ensure a family's compliance with needed services is gaining increasing support from professionals involved in multidisciplinary intervention programs.

Hospitalization, Residential Placement, and Medication. The use of inpatient hospitalization or residential placement as a specific intervention for firesetting behavior has received little attention in the literature, despite the existence of the behavior among a significant percentage of the population (Hanson et al., 1994; Kolko & Kazdin, 1988). It is not uncommon for less-structured hospital units and many residential treatment programs to have written policies that deny admission to any child or adolescent who has a known history of firesetting behavior. Several of my earlier references to treatment interventions that have been developed to address the firesetting behavior of individual juveniles took place within inpatient psychiatric hospital settings (Cox-Jones et al., 1990; Koles & Jenson, 1985; McGrath et al., 1979). However, very few descriptions of interventions and programs that specifically address firesetting behavior within inpatient hospitals or residential treatment centers exist. Geffen (1991) described the development of an inpatient program for compulsive firesetting, which utilized techniques designed to recreate the antecedent conditions and provided the child or adolescent the opportunity to select and practice alternative behaviors to firesetting. DeSalvatore and Hornstein (1991) discussed the application of the "Smokey the Bear" program for 4- to 12-year-old children placed in a short-term, diagnostic unit. The program, delivered in three phases (assessment, didactic, practice), was described as one of the milieu components that sought to improve the child's ego functioning while providing education regarding more adaptive and socially appropriate behaviors. The program describes the application of fire safety educational strategies and behavior modification techniques.

At times the mental health professional is faced with the decision regarding the clinical appropriateness of a juvenile's admission to a more secure residential treatment or inpatient hospital setting. This decision is often necessary when (a) the environment in which the child or adolescent is living is significantly chaotic, unhealthy, or dangerous so as to create an increased level of risk for problematic behaviors or (b) the child's or adolescent's current individual functioning is judged to be unpredictable and dangerous so as to create significant risk of harm to self or others. Gaynor and Hatcher (1987) recommend that the following questions be used to guide the evaluator in their decision making:

1. Is the firesetter planning to set another fire?
2. How specific is the plan in regards to time, place, and materials?
3. Can the youngster make a commitment not to set fires?
4. Can he or she be reasonably expected to keep this promise? Does he or she demonstrate adequate impulse control or judgment?
5. Will the parents cooperate with treatment?

With juveniles whose firesetting behaviors are complex and who remain in crisis states related to unresolved trauma, abuse by parents, and/or personal pathology, there can be increased resistance and hostility towards treatment interventions. The utilization of the structure of the therapeutic milieu, consistent observation, and array of treatment services offered by residential or hospital programs may be necessary for certain children or adolescents who present management problems or are in need of long-term mental health services in addition to a specific firesetting intervention plan. A group of representatives from Massachusetts social service agencies, foster care providers, group home managers, and mental health professionals affiliated with a community-based firesetting program recently developed *The Best Practice Treatment Guidelines for Adolescent Firesetters in Residential Treatment* (Pelletier-Parker et al., 1999). The treatment guidelines are designed to be used by care providers in the development of treatment plans for firesetting youth in substitute care facilities.

There have been no studies that have explored the use of medications and pharmacotherapy as a specific intervention for firesetting behavior. Kolko (1983) cited the use of pharmacotherapy as part of a comprehensive set of services in the treatment of an individual child or adolescent. Depending upon the particular emotional and behavioral symptomatology that a child or an adolescent presents with and consideration of other salient factors related to family and medication management issues, the use of a pharmacotherapy intervention as a component of addressing firesetting risk factors warrants exploration. When appropriately incorporated into a comprehensive set of services, the use of medications that seek to reduce behavioral impulsivity, levels of depressive or anxious feelings, mood lability, or thinking distortions may have a beneficial impact upon a child's or an adolescent's risk for engaging in continued firesetting behavior.

CASE STUDIES

The following case examples are presented to provide the reader with two relevant examples of the demographic, psychological, behavioral, and fire-specific heterogeneity of this population of juveniles involved in firesetting. While the majority of the information provided is taken from actual case data, sufficient details have been altered or eliminated to protect client confidentiality.

"JOSHUA"

Joshua is a 10-year-old boy who was referred for a firesetting evaluation by the clinical staff of his current residential placement. A firesetting incident at his home resulted in Joshua's admission to a local psychiatric hospital. Following discharge from the hospital nearly 2 years earlier, Joshua was placed in the residential program in which he currently resides. The staff now requests a firesetting evaluation in order to assess current level of risk for firesetting behavior and to develop specific recommendations relative to a planned transition back home in the next 6 months.

The data for this evaluation was gathered through the use and application of the following strategies and tools:

Clinical Interviews with Child (2) and Parents (1)
Review of Records/Reports
Developmental Questionnaire
Achenbach Child Behavior Checklist – Parent Form
Firesetting Risk Interview – Parent Form (Kolko)
Achenbach Child Behavior Checklist – Teacher Form
Children's Depression Inventory (CDI)
Children's Firesetting Interview (Kolko)
Projective Drawings
Thematic Apperception Test (TAT)

Background Information. Joshua is a 10-year-old boy who appears to have a treatment history dating back to age 3½, when he was evaluated for problems of impulsivity, hyperactivity, and risk-taking behavior. Joshua's early history, prior to age 7, is remarkable for school behavioral problems; hyperactivity and impulsivity; significant family stress; maternal depression, alcoholism, and panic attacks; sexual abuse by older adolescents; and separations from and conflicts with his father who also has an alcoholism history.

When Joshua was 5, his two infant cousins were killed in a fire, believed to have been electrical in nature. Records note that Joshua's problem behaviors escalated shortly thereafter with reports of increased aggression, suicidal ideation, Tylenol overdose, and intentionally running in front of a car. Joshua's parents were reported to have reconciled shortly after the fatal fire.

Two years later, at age 7, Joshua and his family moved 50 miles to another community. According to parental reports, Joshua's behavior again escalated significantly and Joshua began seeing a counselor as a result of increasing behavior problems at home and school. According to parent reports, Joshua was taken by his intoxicated maternal aunt to the cemetery where his younger cousins were buried. His aunt is reported to have told Joshua that reunification with his dead cousins was possible through death by fire. Joshua's first firesetting behavior occurred 3 weeks after this episode and resulted in a placement in an emergency shelter for 11 days.

Two months later, Joshua's mother was hospitalized for depression and alcoholism and returned home after 1 month. She reports that Joshua lit a second fire, similar to his first fire (see Firesetting Behavior, pp. 69-71), the evening after she returned home from the hospital. Several days later Joshua lit his third fire, which resulted in his emergency psychiatric hospitalization and subsequent placement. After a month-long hospital stay Joshua was transferred to his current treatment program, where during his 20-month placement he has reportedly made significant progress in his behavioral and emotional functioning. A recently completed psychological assessment noted Joshua to be of average intelligence (Full Scale IQ = 104) and at or above grade level for academic skills.

Behavioral Observations/Mental Status Examination. Joshua presented as a pleasant 10-year-old boy who was eager to meet with me and seemingly enjoyed participating in both 90-minute interviews. During each session, however, Joshua displayed significant anxious behaviors. While seated, he would crack his knuckles, bounce on his seat, tap a pencil, and suck and chew on his fingers.

Throughout both interviews Joshua maintained good eye contact and attention. His speech was pressured, resulting in significant stuttering and stammering. Some of Joshua's behaviors appeared to be compulsive attempts to put things in the "right" place, and he seemed very invested in pleasing or performing for this interviewer. He appears to be of average intelligence, and his memory is grossly intact. All perceptual processes were intact with no evidence of thought disorder. Joshua denied visual and auditory hallucinations and reported no current suicidal ideation.

Test Results. Joshua's parents completed the Achenbach Child Behavior Checklist, a 113-item inventory that measures reported behavioral symptoms on nine clinical subscales. Results of the parent form revealed a statistically significant score ($T > 70$) on the "Obsessive-Compulsive" scale ($T = 73$). All other scores were insignificant with only the "Hyperactive" scale approaching significance ($T = 68$). The Teacher's Report Form of the Achenbach Checklist, a 113-item inventory that measures observed behaviors on eight clinical subscales, was completed by the staff of Joshua's school program. Results revealed significant scores ($T > 70$) on the "Obsessive-Compulsive" ($T = 83$) and "Social Withdrawal" ($T = 70$) scales. Scores on the "Nervous-Overactive" ($T = 69$) and "Inattentive" ($T = 68$) approached but did not reach significance.

Joshua completed the Children's Depression Inventory, a 27-item self-report scale of common depression symptoms measured along five subscales, as well as a composite total depression score. None of the self-report scores achieved by Joshua neared significance as T-scores were all within normal limits, with a total depression T-score of 44.

Joshua's parents also completed the 85-item Firesetting Risk Interview, which measures parent concerns and reports of previous firesetting behavior, curiosity, fire safety knowledge, positive and negative behaviors, supervision/discipline, and parental fire awareness. The results of the interview highlighted a tendency of both parents to minimize the importance of the numerous supervision and discipline issues that have been the focus of family therapy. They report significant levels of negative behaviors by Joshua, little confidence in their parenting techniques, and a lack of any formal fire safety training and child fire safety information.

On the Children's Firesetting Interview, a 46-item structured interview involving questions relating to fire involvement, fire knowledge, fire safety skills, and discipline/supervision, Joshua reported high levels of curiosity and interest in learning about fire. He reported low levels of wishes to play with fire, time spent thinking about fire, and excitement about fire. Knowledge of fire safety skills appears average to below average, as is his general fire knowledge. Joshua's performance in this interview was characterized by efforts to provide more detailed an answer than was requested. When he did this, his performance suffered.

Joshua's performance on projective drawings indicates developmental immaturity, a tendency toward impulsivity, and a sense of disappointment and resentment around relationships. Joshua appears in conflict or struggling for control over his impulsive actions and displays some underlying aggression. His projective drawings contain a sense of hopefulness and wishes for nurturance. On the TAT, Joshua displayed what appears to be significant ambivalence, anxiety, and confusion around interpersonal relationships that he fears are potentially dangerous or disappointing. Many of Joshua's stories often described a character who is waiting for ("This kid's playing a harmonica . . . probably waiting for his dad or dog to come.") or unsure about ("I don't know, he's gonna choke him, kill him, or whatever.") relationships. While these are significant fears and concerns, which may create some behavioral disturbances, there is also a sense of hopefulness ("His dad and dog are gonna come home.").

Firesetting Behavior. Given the fact that Joshua's last documented firesetting incident occurred nearly 2 years ago, and that Joshua provided the majority of specific information regarding the incident from memory, the following reports should be interpreted with caution. A comparison of earlier records to reports from his current clinical staff indicate that Joshua has made significant developmental progress since the time of his last fire. This fact will make it somewhat difficult to make specific connections to current functioning.

His parents reported, and Joshua confirmed, the absence of an early history of curiosity, interest, or play with fire. Prior to age 7, Joshua's most significant involvement with fire, which cannot by minimized, was the fire deaths of his two infant cousins when he was 5 years old. Given his history of developmental immaturity and a then age-appropriate understanding of death characterized by magical thinking, it is likely that Joshua was highly suggestible to the pathological thinking of his maternal aunt. Joshua's first firesetting incident, at age 7, occurred within a 6-month period of increased aggression, behavioral problems, and significant family stressors. Joshua denies any specific precipitant to the event and stated that it occurred when he returned home from school one day. He states that he "took paper and stuff from the kitchen trash can, lit it on the stove, and put it out in the kitchen sink." He reports this sequence occurring 3 to 5 times before he was discovered by his mother, who was sitting in the living room at the time (15 feet away). Joshua reports no efforts to hide his behavior from others and is unaware of what the consequences of his actions were. Joshua was subsequently admitted to an emergency shelter program by his therapist as a result of this fire and the other behavioral problems he was experiencing at the time. His actions in this fire suggest significant impulsivity, anxious and compulsive tendencies, and a gross lack of fire safety knowledge. No specific services to address his firesetting behavior were provided at this time.

Shortly after this first firesetting episode, Joshua's mother was hospitalized for concerns around her increasing depression and alcohol abuse. Soon after his mother was discharged from the hospital, Joshua was involved in his second firesetting incident, which was strikingly similar to the first. Again, there is a strong suggestion of some compulsive tendencies in Joshua. Again, the source of ignition was the gas stove, the fuel was trash, and the repetitive nature of an ignition-extinguish sequence was noted. Joshua could not recollect any specific precipitant but did report that he was aware that his mother was in the living room. His mother reported that she discovered Joshua's firesetting behavior when she heard the sound of water spraying in the kitchen. Details regarding parent reaction to this incident were unavailable, and it is unclear if the fire was reported.

Several days later, Joshua, his mother, and his sister overslept, causing the children to miss the bus for school. His mother reports that the family decided to go back to bed at this time. She reports that Joshua went to bed with her although this is inconsistent with his report. Joshua provided all of the following fire scene details, as his mother reported her next recollection as being awakened by Joshua to report the fire.

Joshua states he does not remember going back to bed and was "up and down" from his room (listening to music) and downstairs (watching TV, eating breakfast). He reports that he "saw a candle on the table, lit it on the stove, and brought it upstairs to his parents' room with a calendar from school. He entered his parents' bedroom, ignited the calendar, and "threw it in the closet." When asked why he chose the closet, Joshua reported that he was afraid of the "ghosts" in the closet and thought he could "get rid of them." Joshua's father confirmed in parent interview that Joshua had expressed prior fears of this closet. Joshua reports that he blew out the candle and "walked downstairs."

Joshua returned back upstairs with the candle, after having lit it again, and states he found his father's shirt in the hallway, ignited it, and immediately extinguished it due to fears of his father "getting mean at me." He was unable to identify any motive or intent for returning upstairs and states that he was unaware of the status of the original fire in the closet. After extinguishing the shirt, Joshua states he lit a "tag from a shirt" which he placed at the end of his sister's bed. Joshua reports that he was "angry and jealous" of his sister because "she got attention" and earned rewards from his parents and "I couldn't." Joshua reports that he walked back into his parents' bedroom and discovered the closet on fire and woke his mother immediately. The family escaped from the house and called the fire department immediately. Since this time, Joshua has not expressed an interest in or engaged in any firesetting behavior although he has reported to staff that he has a "fear" of not being able to control his actions. Joshua successfully participated in a fire safety group 6 months ago, and he is reported by the residential program staff to demonstrate more responsible behavior around fire.

Joshua's past firesetting episodes appear to represent the class of firesetting commonly referred to as "crisis" motivated firesetting. These poorly planned, spontaneous, and symbolic fires are typically efforts to communicate distress (crisis) or solve a problem among very immature or nonverbal children. Joshua's firesetting behaviors appear to have occurred during a very stressful period as his acting-out behaviors were symptoms of very significant anxiety and efforts to gain control over his environment. It is realistic to think that the combination of the family's relocation and the resultant stress present in the family resulted in Joshua's overall behavioral escalation. His mother's apparent decline in functioning appears to have served as the primary precipitant to his firesetting behavior. Despite significant program structure and improved family support, Joshua remains highly anxious, suggesting a constitutional or biological anxiety disorder. This anxiety likely exacerbates his impulsive traits and drives his compulsive behaviors and fears. His actions related to the closet fire strongly suggest this anxiety as a primary factor. The anger and jealousy which he reports as motivations for the fire on this sister's bed likely originate from wishes for parental nurturance which, in his eyes, were being continually frustrated. His behaviors and actions also suggest a very immature understanding regarding the dangerousness of fire commonly seen in children up until 5 to 6 years old.

Treatment Recommendations. As a result of the evaluation of Joshua's firesetting behaviors, the following recommendations were developed:

1. Joshua's anxiety and fears are significant, and strong consideration should be given to evaluation for possible medication intervention. This is especially true given the likelihood that a return home will result in increased stress.

2. Joshua's family is in need of significant support from an experienced family therapist to help them manage Joshua's reentry into the home. This therapy should begin prior to Joshua's return home.
3. Joshua's parents should participate in a fire safety education course and request that a fire safety inspection of their home be completed by the fire prevention officer from their local fire department.
4. Joshua should be provided individual therapy to help him manage his significant anxious and fearful feelings.
5. Joshua should complete a fire safety education program that is appropriate to his age.

"CLAUDIA"

Claudia, a 17-year-old Hispanic female, was referred for a firesetting evaluation by the clinical staff of her current residential placement. The evaluation was approved by the state's social services division, her legal guardian. It was hoped that an evaluation of Claudia's involvement in a recent firesetting incident at her last residential placement and a review of her previous firesetting history would aid in the development of recommendations for treatment and disposition planning. In addition, there are current diagnostic questions regarding Claudia due to her past reports of "hearing voices," "dissociation," and "multiple personality disorder," which may suggest the presence of an underlying thought disorder. It is hoped that this evaluation might also clarify some of these diagnostic questions.

The data for this evaluation were gathered through the use and application of the following strategies and tools:

Clinical Interviews (2)
Review of Fire/Police Reports
Review of Records
Achenbach Youth Self-Report
Jesness Inventory
Dissociation Scale
Child/Adolescent Dissociation Checklist (completed by therapist)
Fire Knowledge Pretest
Projective Drawings

Background Information. Claudia is a 17-year-old Hispanic woman whose history prior to age 10 is remarkable for physical abuse by family members, sexual abuse and sexual assault by multiple offenders, exposure to domestic violence, periods of homelessness, chronic school behavioral problems, multiple foster placements, the witnessing of animal abuse, parent incarceration, drug and alcohol use beginning at age 7, and reported maternal neglect. Claudia reports that at age 8 or 9, she joined her first gang "because of my father and Angel (stepfather)."

From age 10 to 11, Claudia was sent to live with her biological father in Costa Rica due to the discovery of physical abuse by her stepfather. Claudia's father had relocated to Costa Rica to escape arrest for several violent offenses. Upon her return to the United States, records indicate that Claudia had been "badly beaten" and required hospitalization. Claudia confirmed in interview that during the year in Costa Rica she was abused by relatives and friends of her father. Claudia was unsure, although doubtful, as to whether her father participated in the abuse and was unable to respond when asked whether her father had attempted to protect her from the abuse. Upon return to the United States at age 11, Claudia reentered her mother's home and reported continued abuse by a second stepfather. Between ages 11 and 12, Claudia reports her involvement in two episodes of firesetting behavior along with her brother David and "some friends."

A review of Claudia's history from ages 12 to 15 indicates the rapid escalation of her involvement in acting out and criminal behavior that was pervasive, self-destructive, violent, and seemingly unremitting. These behaviors included alcohol abuse, drug abuse (cocaine, crack, acid), physical assault, sexual acting out, automobile theft, and gang activity. When asked, Claudia reported that the death of her maternal grandmother was the precipitant for her involvement in these behaviors and that she "wanted revenge on the earth." At age 15 Claudia reports that she joined her second gang "because of this kid, my fiancée," and the gang "took me in." Claudia denies any fire-related behaviors for this 4-year period from ages 12 to 15, and there are no documented reports that suggest otherwise.

This period of time is also remarkable for numerous foster care placements (30) marked by reports of disruptive behaviors by Claudia. Eventually Claudia was determined to be in need of a more secure placement and was placed in a residential treatment program. Claudia's treatment history notes psychiatric hospitalizations at age 14 and 15½ and three residential placements from age 15 to her current placement at age 17. Prior to age 16 there are intermittent notations in the record, confirmed by vague recollections by Claudia, of past reports of "hearing voices," "blacking out," and "dissociating." A review of the records would suggest that several early medication attempts to manage these episodes were either inconclusive or unsuccessful.

Intake and psychiatric notes from Claudia's 5-month placement at the site of her last fire indicate staff concerns regarding dissociative episodes, intrusive thoughts, auditory hallucinations, and mood lability. Claudia's symptoms appeared to lessen after a *reduction* in her antipsychotic medication. Diagnostic summaries at the time noted Post-traumatic Stress Disorder (PTSD; Severe), Borderline Personality Disorder, Dysthymia, and Mood Lability.

In interview Claudia reports that she no longer hears voices, experiences dissociative episodes, or has intrusive thoughts. She reports that this has been true since the referring firesetting incident at her last program and that she has been able to stop the voices through her own volition and willpower. Behavioral observation from staff at her current placement supports these reports. Claudia currently receives no medication support and states she has been drug and alcohol free for 3 months.

Previous cognitive assessments from ages 11 and 13 indicate that Claudia's verbal skills approach the borderline range of intelligence and performance-related skills are low average. It would seem likely that this young woman has a longstanding learning disability, possibly Attention Deficit Disorder, and that her cognitive skills are much lower than average.

Behavioral Observations/Mental Status Examination. Claudia presented as a petite, slim, and cooperative young woman. Her thinking appears clear, as is her speech, and she denies current auditory or visual hallucinations, intrusive thoughts, or dissociative experiences. Her affect is predominantly flat, with angry and slightly paranoid undertones, and she reports chronic interpersonal problems with staff and other residents. Upon entry to first interview Claudia asked, without prompt, "Do you believe everything you read?"

Claudia was cooperative throughout both 2-hour interviews, answering in detail and apologizing to the interviewer for those answers she couldn't provide due to her "forgetting." Claudia displayed fair to poor judgment and insight for someone her age. She denied any suicidal or homicidal ideation.

Test Results. Claudia completed the Achenbach Youth Self-Report, a 112-item behavior rating scale that measures symptomatology along six clinical scales (somatic complaints, depressed, unpopular, thought disorder, aggressive, delinquent). Claudia achieved a clinically significant score ($T = 73$) on the "somatic complaints" scale. No other scores were significant ($T > 70$), with the next highest scores for "aggressive" approaching, but not reaching, significance ($T = 68$).

Claudia completed the Dissociation Scale (Form Three), a 45-item interview which measures the frequency of common dissociative symptoms. Claudia's performance on this scale was insignificant. The majority of items that Claudia reported experiencing were more suggestive of attentional, memory, and impulsive difficulties than disruptions in level of consciousness. Claudia's therapist for the past 6 months completed the Child/Adolescent Dissociation Checklist. The 4 positively endorsed items from the 13-item scale included traumatic history, denial of behavior, physical complaints, and poor learning from experience. A total of 7 positively endorsed items is required to support further evaluation for thought disorder, Multiple Personality Disorder, or dissociative disorders. Claudia was given the 155-item Jesness Inventory to complete. The results were unavailable due to her premature discharge from her placement and relocation.

Claudia's performance on a Fire Knowledge Pretest (37%) was very poor and reflects immature knowledge of fire behavior and safety. When asked to complete with a minimum of 25 words, the following statement, "The reason I set the fire is. . . ," Claudia responded, "I don't know." Her projective drawings suggest that she is an emotionally immature and depressed young lady who struggles with interpersonal relationships and is avoidant of physical stimuli. There are also indications of identity confusion and a sense that those to whom she feels closest are quite distant, if not unavailable, to her. Claudia does report periods of increased interpersonal conflict with other residents and staff. She continues to present in a somewhat paranoid and aggressive manner regarding topics that are relational in nature.

Firesetting Behavior. Claudia reports an extensive history of early exposure to adult firesetting behavior, beginning prior to age 4, and marked by conflicting themes of powerful needs for attachment, control by violence and aggression, and hostile-dependence. Up until age 4 Claudia was an active witness to her biological father's reported frequent firesetting and violent abuse of her mother and siblings. Claudia reports that she believes she was protected from her father's abuse due to her special status ("Daddy's little girl") and by her willingness to comply with her father's demands that she participate in his aggressive firesetting behavior. Claudia reports that she agreed to participate in order to protect her mother and siblings from increased abuse. Claudia states that she and her father participated in "games" related to his firesetting ("hot and cold"). During this early history of extremely disturbed and violent relationships, parental firesetting behavior became confused with issues of attachment, acceptance, trust, violence, control, and abuse. One would expect this to have a direct connection to Claudia's functioning in these areas.

After her father's imprisonment (when Claudia was 4 years old) and her mother's second marriage, Claudia became a victim of both physical and sexual abuse as well as what appears to be continuing maternal deprivation. Claudia appears to have responded by displaying at least two episodes of "crisis motivated" firesetting, involving efforts to communicate her distress through fire-related behavior. These include her detonating a "cherry bomb" in a toilet of her elementary school (4th grade) and setting off a false alarm at the college where she reports her mother was attending night classes. Both of these episodes seem to support the theory of a hostile-dependent motivation for Claudia's involvement with fire.

After her return from Costa Rica at age 11, Claudia reports that she was involved in at least two "delinquent" motivated firesetting episodes involving fires set with her brother and some friends. Claudia has specific recollections of one of the fires being set to "scare a homosexual" who was living in the neighborhood. These are the last reported firesetting behaviors prior to the recent fire, which precipitated this evaluation. Therefore there was a 6-year period of time that was void of any firesetting activity.

There are several factors to note which may have served as immediate precipitants for Claudia's behavior the day of the fire that precipitated her referral. First, Claudia had participated in a sleep-deprived EEG the morning of the fire and had been required to stay awake for the entire evening prior. Second, Claudia reportedly had called her Department of Social Services worker 2 weeks prior to the fire demanding that her placement be changed and had threatened the worker during this conversation. Third, 2 days prior to Claudia's firesetting incident, another resident had set a fire at the residence and had been allowed to return after a 24-hour hospitalization. Claudia reports, and staff members confirm, that she was very angry that this resident was allowed to return. Fourth, the preceding fire resulted in a great amount of attention and discussions occurring among staff and residents regarding fire safety and policies for the several days leading up to Claudia's firesetting incident.

Upon returning from her EEG, Claudia reports that she requested that she be able to do her laundry. Claudia had hidden matches and a cigarette in her laundry — a violation of residence rules — and went into the basement with a magazine. Claudia's reports from this point are sporadic and unreliable. She states that she was disturbed by the contents of a magazine article she was reading (abuse and trauma) and remembers trying to stamp out small pieces of the magazine on the floor. Claudia states that at this point she "dissociated" and remembers very few details. When asked what had been the most powerful impact of her setting the fire, Claudia stated that her biological mother now visits her more frequently than ever before. Claudia reports her mother's reaction as "I never knew how angry you were. I'm sorry for shutting you out of my life."

Reports from the fire scene investigation conducted by arson investigators indicated that Claudia was lighting and throwing matches onto the floor and that the entire magazine was likely placed under a couch in the basement. It would appear that Claudia's intent was to ignite the couch and that she had little knowledge of the explosive behavior of fire. What is equally disturbing is that Claudia was clearly aware that there were other residents and staff in the building and that one resident was bedridden with a serious illness. In addition, when faced with reports by others of smelling smoke prior to discovery of the fire, Claudia did not take any direct action to warn or protect others. While Claudia reported to this interviewer that she did not realize she had lit the fire until 3 or 5 days after the incident, police and fire reports confirm that the day after the fire she told two male residents that she was responsible for it. The final recommendation of the police investigator to the District Attorney was for filing charges of burning a dwelling house. To this date those charges have not proceeded, and the reason for this delay is unclear. Claudia denies any current desire or intent to set a fire and reports, "I learned my lesson."

Claudia's fire history is remarkable for a pattern of behaviors that appear to be efforts on her part to communicate a longing for dependency and nurturance and feelings of great hostility and aggression. Her fires, much like her global personality, reflect a very significant pattern of "hostile-dependency," not atypical of neglect/trauma survivors. Claudia has yet to understand the serious nature of her fire behaviors, especially the most recent episode, and her covert behaviors suggest an effort to avoid taking responsibility for her dangerous actions. This effort also appears to include the intentional feigning of dissociative symptomatology. Claudia's report of her actions and motivation were unreliable, contradicted fire scene evidence, and were characteristic of a much more immature level of functioning than one would expect of a person her age.

Treatment Recommendations. As a result of the evaluation of Claudia's firesetting behaviors, the following recommendations are presented:

1. Claudia's extensive efforts to conceal and avoid the responsibility for her firesetting is of concern and would suggest continued high risk for future dangerous behaviors. Formal and appropriate legal action should be initiated immediately against Claudia for these behaviors.
2. Claudia should be required to remain in a highly structured residential treatment program that can provide the array of intervention services that she requires.
3. Her advanced age and significant learning deficits require the completion of a career/occupational evaluation to determine appropriate goals and programs.
4. Claudia's interpersonal skills are poor, and she should be required to participate in social skills groups to improve her ability to develop and maintain appropriate relationships.
5. Claudia should be provided with individual therapy from a counselor experienced in trauma and abuse.
6. Claudia should be required to successfully complete a formal fire safety education program.

CONCLUSION

Fires set by juveniles in the United States result in an almost incomprehensible amount of property/dollar loss, physically disabling and disfiguring injuries, and emotional/psychological damage. Despite the overwhelming evidence within the public safety/law enforcement community, the public health/medical community, and the insurance industry, juvenile firesetting has received little attention from established mental health organizations. This lack of mental health research, training, and treatment experience, coupled with a history of mythology and misinformation about juvenile firesetting behavior, has created a situation in which interventions designed for firesetting behavior can range from complete minimization to a gross overestimation of a child's or an adolescent's pathology.

The goal of this book is twofold. The first goal is to provide mental health practitioners with an accurate, complete, and research-based source of information regarding juvenile firesetting behavior. In addition to providing historical and descriptive information and assessment and treatment guidelines, I have also furnished contact information for state and national resources for further access to training and/ or multidisciplinary participation opportunities to address this serious problem. The second goal of the book is to motivate and encourage mental health professionals to become more actively involved in such efforts. The trained mental health professional and organized mental health professional groups have an opportunity to play a critical role in multidisciplinary efforts to address juvenile firesetting — one of the greatest public health and safety problems facing juveniles and families.

JUVENILE FIRESETTING RESOURCES

NEWSLETTERS

F.I.R.E.
Indiana State Fire Marshal
402 West Washington Street, #241
Indianapolis, IN 46204
Contact Person: Peggy Zimmer, Editor. Telephone: (317) 232-2226.
(This is a free quarterly newsletter of ideas and information regarding child and adolescent firesetting.)

Hot Issues
Oregon Office of State Fire Marshal
4760 Portland Road NE
Salem, OR 97305-1760
Contact Person: Judith Okulitch, Statewide Coordinator. Telephone: (503) 373-1540. (This quarterly newsletter is available at no cost, and is also available on-line at www.osp.state.or.us/sfm/html/hot-issues.htm. It provides information on the work of the Oregon State Task Force, fire education resources, and national highlights.)

The Strike Zone
Massachusetts Coalition for Juvenile Firesetter Programs
P.O. Box 416
Westport Point, MA 02791
Contact Person: Irene Pinsonneault, Editor. Telephone: (508) 636-9149. (This quarterly newsletter is available at no cost and provides information on fire safety education resources, training opportunities, and recent developments in the child and adolescent firesetting area. It includes articles on assessment, clinical issues, and case summaries.)

NATIONAL AND INTERNATIONAL ORGANIZATIONS

International Association of Arson Investigators (IAAI)
300 South Broadway
St. Louis, MO 63102
(314) 621-1966
http://www.fire-investigators.org

International Association of Fire Chiefs
4025 Fair Ridge Drive, #300
Fairfax, VA 22033

National Fire Protection Association (NFPA)
One Batterymarch Park
Quincy, MA 02269
(617) 770-4543
(617) 770-0200

United States Fire Administration (USFA)
16825 South Seton Avenue
Emmitsburg, MD 21727
(800) 238-3358
http://www.usfa.fema.gov

PROFESSIONAL AND TECHNICAL RESOURCES

Burn Concerns, Inc.
7700 Via Napoli
Burbank, CA 91504
(818) 768-0500

F.I.R.E. Solutions, Inc.
P.O. Box 2888
Fall River, MA 02722
(508) 636-9149

The Ideabank Electronic Catalog
1139 Alameda Padre Serra
Santa Barbara, CA 93103
(800) 621-1136
http://www.theideabank.com

National Fire Service Support Systems
One Grove Street, #210
Pittsford, NY 14534
(716) 264-1754

STATE AND REGIONAL JUVENILE
FIRESETTING INTERVENTION NETWORKS

Bingham Child Guidance Center
200 East Chestnut Street
Louisville, KY 40202
(502) 852-6941

Children's Hospital Burn Center
1056 West Colfax Avenue
Denver, CO 80218
(303) 764-8295

Colorado Division of Fire Safety
700 Kipling Street, Suite 1400
Denver, CO 80215
(303) 239-5704

Connecticut State Fire Academy
P.O. Box 3383
Windsor Locks, CT 06096
(860) 627-6363

Houston Arson Bureau
2802 Louisiana
Houston, TX 77006
(713) 284-1928

Illinois Youthful Firesetter Intervention Association
P.O. Box 12
Plainfield, IL 60544
(708) 496-1268

Kansas State Fire Marshal's Office
700 SW Jackson, Suite #600
Topeka, KS 66603
(785) 296-8436

Massachusetts Coalition for Juvenile Firesetter Intervention Programs
P.O. Box 416
Westport Point, MA 02791
(508) 636-9149

Minnesota State Fire Marshal
444 Cedar Street, #145
St. Paul, MN 55101
(651) 215-1754

New York State Office of Fire Prevention and Control
41 State Street, 12th Floor
Albany, NY 12231
(518) 474-6746

Oregon State Fire Marshal's Office
4760 Portland Road NE
Salem, OR 97305
(503) 378-3473

Phoenix Fire Department-Youth Firesetter Prevention Program
150 South 12th Street
Phoenix, AZ 85034
(602) 262-7712

Utah State Fire Marshal's Office
5272 South College Drive, Suite 302
Murray, UT 84123
(801) 284-6351

Virginia Beach Fire Department
Municipal Center Building
Virginia Beach, VA 23456
(757) 427-4228

REFERENCES

Abidin, R. (1995). *Parental Stress Index.* Odessa, FL: Psychological Assessment Resources.

Achenbach, T., & Edelbrock, C. (1983). *Manual for the Child Behavior Checklist and Revised Child Behavior Profile.* Burlington, VT: University of Vermont, Department of Psychiatry.

Adler, R., Nunn, R., Northam, E., Lebnan, V., & Ross, R. (1994). Secondary prevention of childhood firesetting. *Journal of the American Academy of Child and Adolescent Psychiatry, 33,* 1194-1202.

Alexander, B. (1997). Juvenile arson on steady rise as prevention programs die. *Youth Today, 6*(5), 1-8.

American Psychiatric Association. (1952). *Diagnostic and Statistical Manual of Mental Disorders.* Washington, DC: Author.

American Psychiatric Association. (1968). *Diagnostic and Statistical Manual of Mental Disorders* (2nd ed.). Washington, DC: Author.

American Psychiatric Association. (1980). *Diagnostic and Statistical Manual of Mental Disorders* (3rd ed.). Washington, DC: Author.

American Psychiatric Association. (1987). *Diagnostic and Statistical Manual of Mental Disorders* (3rd ed. rev.). Washington, DC: Author.

American Psychiatric Association. (1994). *Diagnostic and Statistical Manual of Mental Disorders* (4th ed.). Washington, DC: Author.

American Psychological Association. (1992). Ethical principles of psychologists and code of conduct. *American Psychologist, 44,* 1597-1611.

Baizerman, M., & Emshoff, B. (1984). Juvenile firesetting: Building a community based prevention program. *Children Today, May/June,* 8-12.

Barracato, J. S. (1979). *Fire . . . Is It Arson?* Hartford, CT: Aetna Casualty and Surety Company.

Barth, P. (1988). *Social and Cognitive Treatment of Children and Adolescents.* San Francisco: Jossey-Bass.

Briere, J. (1996). *Trauma Symptom Checklist for Children.* Odessa, FL: Psychological Assessment Resources.

Bumpass, E., Brix, R., & Preston, D. (1985). A community based program for juvenile firesetters. *Hospital and Community Psychiatry, 36,* 529-533.

Bumpass, E., Fagelman, F., & Brix, R. (1983). Intervention with children who set fires. *American Journal of Psychotherapy, 37*(3), 328-345.

Campbell, C., & Elliot, E. (1996). *Skills Curriculum for Intervening With Firesetters (Ages 13-18).* Salem, OR: Office of State Fire Marshal.

Carstens, C. (1982). Application of a work penalty threat in the treatment of a case of juvenile fire setting. *Journal of Behavior Therapy and Experimental Psychiatry, 13,* 159-161.

Children's Hospital Burn Center. (1997). *Fire, Kids and Fire Setting.* Denver, CO: Children's Hospital Association.

Clare, I., Murphy, G., Cox, D., & Chapin, E. (1992). Assessment and treatment of firesetting: A single case investigation using a cognitive-behavioral model. *Criminal Behavior, 2,* 253-268.

Cole, R., Grolnick, W., & Schwartzman, P. (1993). Firesetting. In R. Ammerman, C. Last, & M. Hersen (Eds.), *Handbook of Prescriptive Treatments for Children and Adolescents* (pp. 332-346). Boston: Allyn & Bacon.

Conners, C. (1997). *Manual for the Conner's Rating Scale-Revised.* North Tonowanda, NY: Multi-Health Systems.

Cook, R., Hersch, R., Gaynor, J., & Roehl, J. (1989). *The National Juvenile Firesetter/Arson Control and Prevention Program Assessment Report.* Washington, DC: Office of Juvenile Justice and Delinquency Prevention/United States Fire Administration.

Cormier, W., & Cormier, L. (1985). *Interviewing Strategies for Helpers: Fundamental Skills and Cognitive Behavioral Interventions.* Monterey, CA: Brooks/Cole.

Cox-Jones, C., Lubetsky, M., Fultz, S., & Kolko, D. (1990). Inpatient psychiatric treatment of a young recidivist firesetter. *Journal of* the *American Academy of Child and Adolescent Psychiatry, 29,* 936-941.

Dalton, R., Haslett, N., & Daul, G. (1986). Alternative therapy with a recalcitrant fire-setter. *Journal of the American Academy of Child Psychiatry, 25,* 713-717.

DeSalvatore, G., & Hornstein, R. (1991). Juvenile firesetting: Assessment and treatment in psychiatric hospitalization and residential placement. *Child and Youth Care Forum, 20*(2), 103-114.

Egan, G. (1990). *The Skilled Helper: A Systematic Approach to Effective Helping.* Pacific Grove, CA: Brooks/Cole.

Enfield, R. (1987). A model for developing the written forensic report. In P. Keller & S. Heyman (Eds.), *Innovations in Clinical Practice: A Source Book* (Vol. 6, pp. 379-394). Sarasota, FL: Professional Resource Exchange.

Federal Emergency Management Agency. (1979). *Interviewing and Counseling Juvenile Firesetters.* Washington, DC: United States Fire Administration.

Federal Emergency Management Agency. (1983). *Juvenile Firesetters Handbook: Dealing With Children Ages 7-14.* Washington, DC: United States Fire Administration.

Federal Emergency Management Agency. (1988). *Fire in the United States* (7th ed.). Emittsburg, MD: Author.

Fineman, K. (1980). Firesetting in children and adolescents. *Psychiatric Clinics of North America, 3*(3), 483-500.

Fineman, K. (1995). A model for the qualitative analysis of child and adult fire deviant behavior. *American Journal of Forensic Psychology, 13*(1), 31-60.

Forehand, R., Wierson, M., Frame, C., Kempton, T., & Armistead, L. (1991). Juvenile firesetting: A unique syndrome or an advanced level of antisocial behavior? *Behavior Research and Therapy, 29*(2), 125-128.

Freud, S. (1932). The acquisition of power over fire. *International Journal of Psychoanalysis, 13,* 405-410.

Gale, C. M. (1999). *A Survey Study of Incarcerated Male Juveniles With a History of Fire Misuse.* Portland, OR: Morrison Center.

Gaynor, J. (1991). Firesetting. In M. Lewis (Ed.), *Child and Adolescent Psychiatry: A Comprehensive Textbook* (pp. 591-603). Baltimore: Williams and Wilkins.

Gaynor, J., & Hatcher, C. (1987). *The Psychology of Child Firesetting: Detection and Intervention.* New York: Brunner/Mazel.

Gaynor, J., McLaughlin, P., & Hatcher, C. (1984). *The Firehawk's Children's Program: A Working Manual.* San Francisco: National Firehawk Foundation.

Geffen, M. (1991, February 8-9). *Juvenile Firesetting.* Juvenile Firesetters Conference sponsored by The Children's Hospital, Denver, CO, and Joe B. Day and Associates.

Geller, J. (1992). Pathological firesetting in adults. *International Journal of Law and Psychiatry, 15,* 283-302.

Geller, J., McDermeit, M., & Brown, J. (1997). Pyromania? What does it mean? *Journal of Forensic Science, 42,* 1052-1057.

Grolnick, W., Cole, R., Laurenitis, L., & Schwartzman, P. (1990). Playing with fire: A developmental assessment of children's fire understanding and experience. *Journal of Clinical Child Psychology, 19,* 128-135.

Gruber, A., Heck, T., & Mintzer, E. (1981). Children who set fires: Some background and behavioral characteristics. *American Journal of Orthopsychiatry, 51,* 484-488.

Hall, J. (1995). *Children Playing With Fire: U.S. Experience 1980-1993.* Quincy, MA: National Fire Protection Association.

Hall, J. (1997). *Patterns of Fire Casualties in Home Fires by Age and Sex.* Quincy, MA: National Fire Protection Association.

Hanson, M., Mackay, S., Atkinson, L., Staley, S., & Pignatiello, A. (1995). Firesetting during the preschool period: Assessment and intervention issues. *Canadian Journal of Psychiatry, 40*(4), 299-303.

Hanson, M., Mackay-Soroka, S., Staley, S., & Poulton, L. (1994). Delinquent firesetters: A comparative study of delinquency and firesetting histories. *Canadian Journal of Psychiatry, 39*(4), 230-232.

Harris, G., & Rice, M. (1996). A typology of mentally disordered firesetters. *Journal of Interpersonal Violence, 11*(3), 351-363.

Heath, G., Hardesty, V., Goldfine, P., & Walker, A. (1985). Diagnosis and childhood firesetting. *Journal of Clinical Psychology, 41,* 571-575.

Hollin, C. (1990). *Cognitive-Behavioural Interventions With Young Offenders.* Elmsford, NY: Pergamon Press.

Houston Fire Department. (1998). *Cleared Child Arson Log.* Houston, TX: Author.

Humphreys, J., & Kopet, T. (1996). *Manual for Juvenile Firesetter Needs Assessment Protocol.* Portland, OR: Oregon State Fire Marshal.

Humphreys, J., Kopet, T., & Lajoy, R. (1996). *Guidelines for Caregivers of Juvenile Firesetters.* Portland, OR: Oregon State Fire Marshal.

Jayaprakash, S., Jung, J., & Panitch, D. (1984). Multi-factorial assessment of hospitalized children who set fires. *Child Welfare, 63,* 74-78.

Jesness, C. (1996). *The Jesness Inventory Manual.* North Tonowanda, NY: Multi-Health Systems.

Jones, F. (1981). Therapy for firesetters [Letter to the Editor]. *American Journal of Psychiatry, 138,* 261-262.

Kafry, D. (1980). Playing with matches: Children and fire. In D. Canter (Ed.), *Fires and Human Behavior* (pp. 47-61). Chichester, England: Wiley and Sons.

Kazdin, A. (1997). Practitioner review: Psychological treatments for conduct disorder in children. *Journal of Child Psychology and Psychiatry, 38,* 161-178.

Kazdin, A., & Kolko, D. (1986). Parent psychopathology and family functioning among childhood firesetters. *Journal of Abnormal Child Psychology, 14*(2), 315-329.

Koles, M., & Jenson, W. (1985). Comprehensive treatment of chronic fire setting in a severely disordered boy. *Journal of Behavior Therapy and Experimental Psychiatry, 16,* 81-85.

Kolko, D. (1983). Multicomponent parental treatment of firesetting in a developmentally disabled boy. *Journal of Behavior Therapy and Experimental Psychiatry, 14,* 349-353.

Kolko, D. (1985). Juvenile firesetting: A review and methodological critique. *Clinical Psychology Review, 5,* 345-376.

Kolko, D. (1988). Community interventions for juvenile firesetters: A survey of two national programs. *Hospital and Community Psychiatry, 39,* 973-979.

Kolko, D. (1989). Firesetting and pyromania. In C. Last & M. Hersen (Eds.), *Handbook of Child Psychiatric Diagnosis* (pp. 443-459). New York: Wiley and Sons.

Kolko, D. (1996). Education and counseling for child firesetters: A comparison of skills training programs with standard practice. In E. Hibbs & P. Jensen (Eds.), *Psychosocial Treatments for Child and Adolescent Disorders: Empirically Based Strategies for Clinical Practice* (pp. 409-433). Washington, DC: American Psychological Association.

Kolko, D. (1999a). Firesetting in children and youth. In V. Van Hasselt & M. Hersen (Eds.), *Handbook of Psychological Approaches With Violent Offenders: Contemporary Strategies and Issues* (pp. 95-115). New York: Kluwar Academic/Plenum Publishers.

Kolko, D. (1999b, November). *Children and Fire VI.* Paper presented at the Institute on Clinical Treatment Conference, Westford, Massachusetts.

Kolko, D., & Ammerman, R. (1988). Firesetting. In M. Hersen & C. Last (Eds.), *Child Behavior Therapy Casebook* (pp. 243-262). New York: Plenum.

Kolko, D., & Kazdin, A. (1986). A conceptualization of firesetting in children and adolescents. *Journal of Abnormal Child Psychology, 14*(1), 49-61.

Kolko, D., & Kazdin, A. (1988). Prevalence of firesetting and related behaviors among child psychiatric patients. *Journal of Consulting and Clinical Psychology, 56*(4), 628-630.

Kolko, D., & Kazdin, A. (1989a). Assessments of dimensions of childhood firesetting among patients and nonpatients: The firesetting risk interview. *Journal of Abnormal Child Psychology, 17*(2), 157-176.

Kolko, D., & Kazdin, A. (1989b). The children's firesetting interview with psychiatrically referred and nonreferred children. *Journal of Abnormal Child Psychology, 17,* 609-624.

Kolko, D., & Kazdin, A. (1990). Matchplay and firesetting in children: Relationship to parent, marital, and family dysfunction. *Journal of Clinical Child Psychology, 19*(3), 229-238.

Kolko, D., & Kazdin, A. (1991a). Aggression and psychopathology in matchplay and firesetting children: A replication and extension. *Journal of Clinical Child Psychology, 20*(2), 191-201.

Kolko, D., & Kazdin, A. (1991b). Motives of childhood firesetters: Firesetting characteristics and psychological correlates. *Journal of Child Psychology and Psychiatry, 32*(3), 535-550.

Kolko, D., Watson, S., & Faust, J. (1991). Fire safety/Prevention skills training to reduce involvement with fire in young psychiatric inpatients: Preliminary findings. *Behavior Therapy, 22,* 269-284.

Kuhnley, E., Hendren, R., & Quinland, D. (1982). Firesetting by children. *Journal of American Academy of Child Psychiatry, 21,* 560-563.

Last, C., Griest, D., & Kazdin, A. (1985). Physiological and cognitive assessment of a fire-setting child. *Behavior Modification, 9*(1), 94-102.

Lewis, D., Shanok, S., Pincus, J., & Glaser, G. (1980). Violent juvenile delinquents: Psychiatric, neurological, psychological and abuse factors. *Annals of Programs in Child Psychiatry and Child Development,* pp. 591-603.

Lewis, N., & Yarnell, H. (1951). Pathological fire-setting (pyromania). *Nervous and Mental Disease* (Monograph No. 82). New York: Coolidge Foundation.

Lochman, J. (1992). Cognitive-behavioral intervention with aggressive boys: Three year follow-up and preventive effects. *Journal of Consulting and Clinical Psychology, 60,* 426-432.

Lowenstein, L. (1981). The diagnosis of child arsonists. *Acta Paedopsychiatrica, 47*(1), 151-154.

Mahoney, J. (1999, November). *Children and Fire VI.* Paper presented at the Institute on Clinical Treatment Conference, Westford, Massachusetts.

Massachusetts Coalition for Juvenile Firesetter Intervention Programs (Irene Pinsonneault, Editor). (1999). *Children and Fire: Annual Report for 1999.* Fall River, MA: Author.

McGrath, P., Marshall, P., & Prior, P. (1979). A comprehensive treatment program for a fire setting child. *Journal of Behavioral Therapy and Experimental Psychiatry, 10,* 69-72.

Moore, J., Thompson-Pope, K., & Whited, R. (1996). MMPI-A profiles of adolescent boys with a history of firesetting. *Journal of Personality Assessment, 67*(1), 116-126.

National Center for Health Statistics. (1984). *Monthly Vital Statistics.* Washington, DC: U.S. Government Printing Office.

National Fire Protection Association. (1992). *Learn Not to Burn* (3rd ed.). Quincy, MA: Author.

National Fire Protection Association. (1997). *Facts About Fire: Fire Loss in the United States and Canada.* Quincy, MA: Author.

National Fire Protection Association. (1998). *1992-1996 NFIRS and NFPA Survey.* Quincy, MA: Author.

Oregon State Fire Marshal. (1996). *Children and Fire: A Report on Oregon's Juvenile Firesetter Intervention Program.* Salem, OR: Author.

Oregon Treatment Strategies Task Force. (1996). *The Cycles of Firesetting: An Oregon Model.* Salem, OR: Oregon State Fire Marshal.

Pelletier-Parker, A., Slate, F., Morirarty, D., & Pinsonneault, I. (1999). *The Best Practice Treatment Guidelines for Adolescent Firesetters in Residential Treatment.* Boston, MA: Option/Commonworks.

Perry, G., & Orchard, J. (1992). *Assessment and Treatment of Adolescent Sex Offenders.* Sarasota, FL: Professional Resource Press.

Phoenix Fire Department. (1999). *Youth Firesetter Intervention Program.* Phoenix, AZ: Author.

Pierce, J., & Hardesty, V. (1997). Non-referral of psychopathological child firesetters to mental health services. *Journal of Clinical Psychology, 53*(4), 349-350.

Pinsonneault, I., & Richardson, J. (1989a). *The F.I.R.E. Manual.* Warwick, RI: F.I.R.E. Solutions.

Pinsonneault, I., & Richardson, J. (1989b). *The F.I.R.E. Protocol: An Assessment Instrument for Firesetting Behaviors.* Warwick, RI: F.I.R.E. Solutions.

Porth, D. (1997). *Juvenile Firesetting: A Four Year Perspective.* Portland, OR: SOS Fires Youth Intervention Program.

Quinsey, V., Chaplin, T., & Upfold, D. (1989). Arsonists and sexual arousal to fire setting: Correlation unsupported. *Journal of Behavioral Therapy and Experimental Psychiatry, 20*(3), 203-209.

Raines, J., & Foy, C. (1994). Extinguishing the fires within: Treating juvenile firesetters. *The Journal of Contemporary Human Services, 75,* 595-606.

Ray, I. (1838). *A Treatise on the Medical Jurisprudence of Insanity.* Boston: C. C. Thomas and J. Brown.

Ray, I. (1844). *A Treatise on the Medical Jurisprudence of Insanity* (4th ed.). Boston: Little Brown and Co.

Reis, L. (1993). *Family Functioning of Firesetters, Antisocial Firesetters, and Nonproblem Adolescents.* Published doctoral dissertation, Texas Women's University, Denton, TX.

Reynolds, C., & Kamphaus, R. (1996). *Manual for the Behavior Assessment System for Children (BASC).* Circle Pines, MN: American Guidance Service.

Rice, M., & Harris, G. (1991). Firesetters admitted to a maximum security psychiatric institution: Offenders and offenses. *Journal of Interpersonal Violence, 6,* 461-475.

Ritvo, E., Shanok, S., & Lewis, D. (1982). Firesetting and nonfiresetting delinquents: A comparison of neuropsychiatric, psychoeducational, experiential, and behavioral characteristics. *Child Psychiatry and Human Development, 13,* 259-267.

Roberts, G., Schmitz, K., Pinto, J., & Cain, S. (1990). The MMPI and Jesness Inventory as measures of effectiveness on an inpatient conduct disorders treatment unit. *Adolescence, 25,* 989-996.

Sakheim, G., & Osborn, E. (1994). *Firesetting Children: Risk Assessment and Treatment.* Washington, DC: Child Welfare League of America.

Sakheim, G., Osborn, E., & Abrams, D. (1991). Toward a clearer differentiation of high-risk from low-risk firesetters. *Child Welfare, 70*(4), 489-503.

Saunders, E. B., & Awad, G.A. (1991). Adolescent female firesetters. *Canadian Journal of Psychiatry, 36*(6), 401-404.

Showers, J., & Pickrell, E. (1987). Child firesetters: A study of three populations. *Hospital and Community Psychiatry, 38,* 495-501.

Snyder, H. N. (1998). *Juvenile Arson, 1997* (Office of Juvenile Justice and Delinquency Prevention Fact Sheet #91). Washington, DC: U.S. Department of Justice.

Stadolnik, R. (1998a, May). *Child/Juvenile Firesetting Behavior.* Paper presented at New Hampshire Division for Children, Youth, and Families Conference, Nashua, NH.

Stadolnik, R. (1998b, November). *Master Class: Treatment Planning for the Child/Juvenile Firesetter.* Paper presented at Massachusetts Coalition for Juvenile Firesetter Intervention Programs Conference, Framingham, MA.

Stadolnik, R. (1999). Child and juvenile firesetting behavior: Psychology moves from myth to facts. *Massachusetts Psychological Association Quarterly, 42*(4), 8-16.

Steinbach, G. (1986). Les differentes conceptionss du droit en matiere d'incendie et les generalites criminologiques sur les incendiarires. *Neuropsychiatricc de l'Enfance et de l'Adolescence, 34,* 33-38.

Stekel, W. (1924). *Peculiarities of Behavior.* New York: Boni & Liveright.

Swaffer, T., & Hollin, C. (1995). Adolescent firesetting: Why do they say they do it? *Journal of Adolescence, 18,* 619-623.

Vreeland, R., & Waller, M. (1979). *Personality Theory and Firesetting: An Elaboration of a Psychological Model.* Washington, DC: U.S. Department of Commerce.

Webb, N., Sakheim, G., Towns-Miranda, L., & Wagner, C. (1990). Collaborative treatment of juvenile firesetters: Assessment and outreach. *American Journal of Orthopsychiatry, 60,* 305-310.

Webster's Ninth New Collegiate Dictionary. (1986). Springfield, MA: Merriam-Webster, Inc.

Winget, C., & Whitman, R. (1973). Coping with problems: Attitudes towards children who set fires. *American Journal of Psychiatry, 130,* 442-445.

Wooden, W., & Berkey, M. (1984). *Children and Arson: America's Middle Class Nightmare.* New York: Plenum.

Yudofsky, S. (1986). The overt aggression scale for the objective rating of verbal and physical aggression. *American Journal of Psychiatry, 143,* 35-39.

Zingaro, J., & Pittman-Wagers, J. (1992). The use of hypnosis in the treatment of a child firesetter. *Journal of Strategic and Systemic Therapies, 11,* 63-71.

If You Found This Book Useful . . .

You might want to know more about our other titles.

If you would like to receive our latest catalog, please return this form:

Name:_____
                        (Please Print)

Address:_____

Address:_____

City/State/Zip:_____
                        This is ❏ home ❏ office

Telephone:(_____)_____

I am a:

_____ Psychologist   _____ Mental Health Counselor
_____ Psychiatrist   _____ Marriage and Family Therapist
_____ School Psychologist   _____ Not in Mental Health Field
_____ Clinical Social Worker   _____ Other:_____

◆   ◆   ◆

Professional Resource Press
P.O. Box 15560
Sarasota, FL 34277-1560

Telephone: 800-443-3364
FAX: 941-343-9201
E-mail: mail@prpress.com
Website: http://www.prpress.com

Add A Colleague To Our Mailing List . . .

If you would like us to send our latest catalog to one of your colleagues, please return this form.

Name:_____
                        (Please Print)

Address:_____

Address:_____

City/State/Zip:_____
                        This is ☐ home ☐ office

Telephone:(_____)_____

This person is a:

_____ Psychologist   _____ Mental Health Counselor
_____ Psychiatrist   _____ Marriage and Family Therapist
_____ School Psychologist   _____ Not in Mental Health Field
_____ Clinical Social Worker   _____ Other:_____

Name of person completing this form:_____

◆　　　◆　　　◆

Professional Resource Press
P.O. Box 15560
Sarasota, FL 34277-1560

Telephone: 800-443-3364
FAX: 941-343-9201
E-mail: mail@prpress.com
Website: http://www.prpress.com

DTF/7/00